THE
INSIDE
ADVANTAGE

THE INSIDE ADVANTAGE

The Strategy That Unlocks the Hidden Growth in Your Business

ROBERT H. BLOOM

with Dave Conti

New York   Chicago   San Francisco
Lisbon   London   Madrid   Mexico City   Milan
New Delhi   San Juan   Seoul   Singapore
Sydney   Toronto

The **McGraw·Hill** *Companies*

Copyright © 2008 by Robert H. Bloom. All rights reserved. Printed in the United States of America. Except as permitted under the United States Copyright Act of 1976, no part of this publication may be reproduced or distributed in any form or by any means, or stored in a data base or retrieval system, without the prior written permission of the publisher.

1 2 3 4 5 6 7 8 9 0   DOC/DOC   0 9 8 7

ISBN-13: 978-0-07-149569-1
ISBN-10: 0-07-149569-X

McGraw-Hill books are available at special quantity discounts to use as premiums and sales promotions, or for use in corporate training programs. For more information, please write to the Director of Special Sales, Professional Publishing, McGraw-Hill, Two Penn Plaza, New York, NY 10121-2298. Or contact your local bookstore.

This book is printed on acid-free paper.

CONTENTS

INTRODUCTION: Your Inside Advantage Is the
Key to Growth 1

PART 1: CORE CUSTOMERS
WHO Are They?

CHAPTER 1   The Most Important Word in
Business 13

CHAPTER 2   All Customers Are Not Created
Equal 27

CHAPTER 3   Zero In on Your Core Customer 41

PART 2: UNCOMMON OFFERINGS
WHAT Can You Offer Them?

CHAPTER 4   What Business Are You *Really* In? 59

CHAPTER 5   Where Tangible Meets Emotional 83

CHAPTER 6   Dig Deep for Your Advantage 95

PART 3: PERSUASIVE STRATEGIES
HOW Do You Convince Them?

CHAPTER 7   A Platform Built for One 111

CHAPTER 8   Stand Out by Standing Alone 123

CHAPTER 9   Create a Compelling Persuasive
Strategy 133

PART 4: IMAGINATIVE ACTS
        OWN IT!

CHAPTER 10   Never Stop Celebrating
             Your Advantage 149

CHAPTER 11   Ubiquitous and Explosive Acts 173

CHAPTER 12   Become Well Known for
             Your Advantage 179

CONCLUSION: Make Growth Happen—NOW! 203

        Notes 211

        Index 215

THE
INSIDE
ADVANTAGE

Your Inside Advantage Is the Key to Growth

Grow or die! Every businessperson must understand this stark reality. In today's intensely competitive, technology-driven global marketplace, no enterprise—including yours—can be sustained without growth.

In fact, I believe that a flourishing business should double in size every five years. It's an ambitious goal but at the same time a reasonable measure of an aggressively managed firm, firing on all cylinders, on track to reach its full potential.

Although the task may seem daunting, it doesn't have to be. I've developed an easier and better way to promote healthy growth in a business—a unique approach that stems from my 45-year career as an entrepreneur and a corporate CEO. My way capitalizes on a strategic asset that is already present in the company. You see, it's been my experience that every enterprise has at least one underutilized existing strength that can be the centerpiece of a powerful growth strategy. This unexploited strength is often hidden

1

deep inside the firm, waiting to be discovered and put to work. When it is, it becomes your business's Inside Advantage.

The approach works because it's single-minded, uncomplicated, and practical. As the pages of this book will reveal, I've proved that it works—my businesses and my clients' businesses have prospered because of it. Finding and using the Inside Advantage in your business will enable you to prosper too.

BLOOM ON GROWTH

In today's intensely competitive, technology-driven global marketplace, no enterprise–including yours–can be sustained without growth.

If you follow the course of action I've laid out in this book, you will evaluate your firm's inventory of *special* ideas, products, services, processes, or ways of working, and identify your most marketable strength. You will use this valuable strategic asset to jump-start sales, motivate customer loyalty, and generate profits for your business no matter what its size or industry.

I'll show you how to do all this by using an uncomplicated four-step method that I call the Growth Discovery Process. My process will enable you to find your hidden strength, nourish it, and become well known for it. When this happens you will unlock your Inside Advantage and grow your business.

The Growth Discovery Process is the product of my experience in helping global corporations, famous brands, and entrepreneurial firms in a wide variety of industries capitalize on their Inside Advantage. This is not academic theory from a university professor. It's not complex methodology from a high-priced consultant. It's certainly not a lesson in leadership from a motivational expert. It is a practical, systematic approach to business growth that's demonstrated on page after page of this book. It's an easy-to-use and simple-to-apply process that will enable you to discover and leverage your Inside Advantage—and grow.

It's important to understand that all growth is not created equal. Sales growth is essential to assure that revenue exceeds the company's ever-increasing cost of doing business. And, to ensure the company's enduring health and prosperity, profits must grow in step with or even faster than revenue. Sacrificing profits with excessively ambitious plans—such as unrealistic expansion, expensive acquisitions, extravagant marketing, and unrelated new products or services—often ends up killing the company instead.

Even worse, some business leaders can't resist the seductive exhortation to "reinvent" their businesses—to turn them into something that they do not have the potential to be. This often unrealistic promise of "profound transformation" consumes precious time and resources—and it usually fails because it destroys the heart and soul of the original enterprise.

My approach to growth, as you've probably figured out already, is very different. It begins with this simple principle:

The best way to expand the size, scope, and profit of your business is to grow it from the inside, capitalizing on hidden strengths that already exist within the company or brand.

Why do I have such faith in this approach? And why should you believe me?

The answer is that it has worked for me throughout my career, and I know it will work for you.

BLOOM ON GROWTH

Even worse, some business leaders can't resist the seductive exhortation to "reinvent" their businesses—to turn them into something that they do not have the potential to be.

It worked for me as I built the small advertising firm in Dallas, Texas, that my dad and mentor Sam R. Bloom founded, into a large, successful national agency. Instead of apologizing for our then out-of-the-mainstream location, we celebrated it and turned it into our Inside Advantage.

This growth principle worked again as I helped Publicis Groupe grow into one of the largest advertising and communications companies in the world. My mission was defined by the brilliant, ambitious Global Chairman/CEO of Publicis Groupe SA, Maurice Levy, who constantly reminded me of this profound insight about growth, one that he recently repeated in an interview with CNN: "No one stays small because of his goodwill. It's not by his goodwill that he stays small; it's because he cannot grow. So if we grow it will be because we are very good, because we are the best." During my tenure as CEO of Publicis USA, I quadrupled revenue, expanded to 12 domestic offices, managed a staff of over 1,000, and developed a roster of world-class clients such as L'Oréal, BMW, Nestlé, Siemens, T.G.I. Friday's, Whirlpool, Fujifilm, T-Mobile, and many others.

And it worked again as I applied my growth concept to clients' businesses, devising strategies to generate profitable growth for their brands, products, and services.

I'd like to take you back for a moment to the beginning of my career in Texas and the genesis of my approach to growth. I wasn't born in a corporate suit—I began in business as a frustrated entrepreneur, worrying about our growth-starved 12-employee ad agency. In searching for ways to stimulate the business, I came to realize that our greatest strength, our hidden potential, was staring me right in the face—our Texas location. At the time, we were in the center of the rapidly growing "Sunbelt" region of the United States. Dallas was a virtual boomtown, and we were riding its crest.

Our ad agency's Inside Advantage was the firsthand knowledge we possessed of the unique Sunbelt region and its people, and our proven ability to create campaigns that worked extremely well there. I used this reputation to win clients headquartered outside our home region who wanted to grow their Sunbelt brands.

For example, we were hired by the fledgling Marriott Corporation to launch a hotel it was building in Dallas—the first hotel outside the company's Washington, D.C., home office region. It was then that I met J. W. Marriott, Sr., who started his distinguished career serving up hamburgers in a small family food stand near the D.C. airport. As the assignment progressed, I worked closely with J. W. (Bill) Marriott, Jr., who used his entrepreneurial genes to build a global hotel empire. The Marriott family hospitality was and still is the company's Inside Advantage.

There were plenty of other national companies that needed our specialization to grow their smaller Sunbelt brands. Our Inside Advantage got us in the door of many companies with large portfolios of brands that we could grow with. Our initial assignment from Block Drug Company was an analgesic product marketed exclusively in the Southeast. This led to our assignment of Block's national PoliGrip and Beano brands. We won Libby's line of canned meats, a Nestlé brand with heavy consumption in the southern part of the country. This led to our assignment of Nestlé's national Juicy Juice brand, ice cream products, and Power Bar brand. Throughout the book, you'll read much more about how we located and leveraged the Inside Advantage in these businesses, achieving success for them and our agency.

In 1971, our agency was hired to launch Southwest Airlines. As the airline had no offices at that time, many of its first employees were recruited in our Dallas office. We were able to observe the company's corporate culture up close from day one. We realized that the managers and employees had something we'd never observed in another airline: a fun-loving, love-the-customer attitude. We felt that this attitude, if truly carried out in all of its operations and contacts with customers, could well be Southwest's Inside Advantage. We crafted our marketing and advertising approach to communicate this perceptible passenger benefit. The airline adopted and nourished this company culture, consistently providing a friendly face to its customers. Southwest is now one of the largest airlines in the nation and one of the world's most successful. The success of our Southwest campaign put our agency in the national spotlight.

I put my Inside Advantage principle to use again when our agency acquired a New York agency and then found itself in fierce competition with big, firmly entrenched, New York–based national and international agencies. In order to succeed in this vastly larger playing field, we needed a growth strategy. Examining our strengths, looking for the hidden potential, I realized that it lay in our ability to plan and implement new product launches faster and better than our lumbering competitors. That was what set us apart. That was our Inside Advantage.

We capitalized on the stunning success of our New York agency's U.S. introduction of a small green bottle of fizzy water from France called Perrier. This well-publicized achievement showcased our specialization in the new products arena. We lived and breathed new products, aligning all aspects of our agency to it, and coupling it with a sense of urgency and more top management involvement than our giant competitors could muster. We sought and landed new products assignments from larger and larger clients, such as the Swiss drug giant Sandoz (now Novartis), who awarded us its Theraflu, Triaminic, and Tavist brands. That was our growth strategy, and it worked. We emerged as a fast-growing national agency.

My special contribution then and now is my ability to find a company's Inside Advantage—to identify the unique strength hiding in a business and to use this strength to grow the business. Throughout the book, you'll find a great many examples of this strategic concept at work, including:

- Start-up companies such as a fitness center and an upscale tanning salon chain

- Struggling small companies such as a regional wealth management firm and a sports and entertainment marketing agency

- Rapidly expanding medium-size B2B firms such as a financial publishing company and a technology provider to international communication firms

- Large national brands like Zales jewelers, T.G.I. Friday's, and T-Mobile

- Famous international brands such as Nestlé, BMW, and L'Oréal

- Fascinating business situations from all parts of the world from companies like the German giant Siemens and the Chinese dairy giant Mengniu.

I've written this book for hardworking, time-constrained people like you who know your craft but don't necessarily know how to craft a growth strategy. If you want to do what I did—take your business or brand and make it better, bigger, and stronger— then please examine the process carefully and learn how to put your Inside Advantage to work:

The Growth Discovery Process

WHO + WHAT + HOW + OWN IT! = INSIDE ADVANTAGE

WHO is the *core customer* most likely to buy your product or service in the quantity required for optimal profit.

WHAT is the *uncommon offering* that your business will own and leverage.

HOW is the *persuasive strategy* that will convince your *core customer* to buy your *uncommon offering* versus all competitive offerings.

OWN IT! is the series of *imaginative acts* that will celebrate your *uncommon offering* and make it well known to your *core customer*.

As you can see, the process has only four components—
WHO, WHAT, HOW, and **OWN IT!** Throughout the book, you'll
find the language of the process easy to understand and apply to
your own business. Using it always stimulates the imagination of my
clients, shifting it into high gear. I know it will do the same for you.
But please don't be tempted to get to work on it right away. Let me
guide you through it in the course of the book.

Each part of the book corresponds to the steps in the Growth
Discovery Process. In Part 1, *Core Customers*, you'll determine your
target audience. In Part 2, *Uncommon Offerings*, you'll uncover the
essence of the benefits you offer customers. And in Part 3,
Persuasive Strategies, you'll develop an approach to convince customers to buy from you, not your competitor. In all, these roll up
into a sound strategic framework for your Inside Advantage.

Once this framework is in place, we move on to Part 4,
Imaginative Acts, where you'll learn how to generate a roster of
inventive activities to establish and maintain a reputation based on
your *uncommon offering*. This series of creative ways to reinforce
and highlight your Inside Advantage will enable your company or
brand to be well known to customers and prospects alike.

Throughout the book I'll illustrate the process in action using
numerous examples drawn from my client files. These are clients I
worked with intimately as I helped them shape their business
growth plans.

I'll discuss lessons I learned from Stanley Marcus, the legendary founder of Neiman Marcus; Robert Dotson, the aggressive
and passionate CEO of T-Mobile; Marc Bourgery, the inventive
strategic planner from Publicis; and other great minds from the
business world with whom I've worked. You'll get a close, firsthand,
down-in-the-trenches understanding of how successful companies
leverage their hidden strengths to grow their businesses.

By the time you finish reading this book, you'll be rewarded
with a powerful growth strategy. You'll have discovered profound

new insight into the core values of your business. You'll develop a clear understanding of who your customers are, what your offering to those customers should be, how to persuade customers to buy from you rather than from competitors, and how to become well known for your Inside Advantage. You will come away with a new and deeper understanding of the fundamental nature of your business and of its primary strategic assets.

Finally, I'll guide you in the writing of an enduring clarifying statement for each of the four parts of the Growth Discovery Process, resulting in a concise 40- or 50-word "blueprint" that will be the centerpiece of your growth strategy. By following my process to its completion, you'll have in your possession a dynamic growth strategy with imaginative tactics ready to implement immediately. Consider it an internal strategic blueprint for the growth of your business and a rallying cry for your entire organization. Your customers won't see it, but they will certainly feel its effects.

> **BLOOM ON GROWTH**
>
> Right now—somewhere *inside your business*—there are growth-generating customer benefits waiting to ignite your enterprise.

You'll find a number of FAQs—frequently asked questions—placed at the end of each part of the book where they can assist you in applying what you've just learned. They are specifically dedicated to helping you work through the statement writing process. So save up your questions and you'll probably find your answers there.

No matter what the size of your business or its nature, the Growth Discovery Process will clarify your vision, focus your goals, refresh your entrepreneurial spirit, and set you firmly on the road to growth. These seeds of growth are close at hand—much closer than perhaps you've ever realized. This is true whether you own a small business, run a corporate division or department, manage a brand, or direct a nonprofit organization. In fact, right now—somewhere *inside your business*—there are growth-generating customer benefits waiting to ignite your enterprise.

Running a successful business is more challenging than ever. Globalization and the Internet change everything, repeatedly. Markets evolve and dissolve more rapidly than ever. Each year, almost 600,000 U.S. companies close their doors, but in the same year another 600,000 open theirs. In many Asian and emerging economies, businesses face still other barriers—vast bureaucracies and cultures of graft. In India, the 12 million "mom and pop" stores must brace for the far-reaching effects of Wal-Mart's decision to open hundreds of giant stores there. Even in the highly developed economies of Europe, growth difficulties exist—France enjoys a strong record on company start-ups, but growth remains significantly lower than in the United States. Almost half of all U.K. businesses that started between 2001 and 2002 are not around. Growing any business anywhere is challenging, but it's also one of the most satisfying and rewarding experiences in the world, and I want to help you grow yours by discovering its Inside Advantage.

Let's get started.

Core
Customers

WHO Are They?

CHAPTER 1

The Most Important Word in Business

As a corporate manager, a business owner, or an entrepreneur, you are intimately involved with all aspects of your business. You know everything there is to know about your products, services, employees, costs, and competitors. You live your business 24/7.

You talk to your customers every day—and when you don't, you are reviewing sales reports, learning about customer reactions to your products and services, and, I hope, examining the entire transaction experience with your firm.

You pore over every piece of demographic information you can lay your hands on: data from trade associations and community and government agencies as well as the charts and graphs in the original studies your company has initiated. You know that any current, reliable insights into the profiles of your customer or potential customer will prove valuable in growing your business.

But after all that, do you really know your customer?

I believe that *customer* is the most important word in the vocabulary of business.

That's why the first step in my Growth Discovery Process focuses on your *core customer*, your target for all future growth. You can't leverage your Inside Advantage, you can't grow, you can't even survive in business, if you don't recognize that customers and potential customers are paramount and that there is far more to them than a statistic can convey.

If you are convinced that you know everything you need to know about your customers—perhaps this story will convince you otherwise.

Procter & Gamble (P&G), one of the largest, most profitable consumer products companies, recently introduced its highly successful Swiffer Wet Mop in Italy. According to the *Wall Street Journal*, P&G conducted research that revealed that Italian women keep very clean houses, in fact spending an average of 21 hours each week on household chores—not counting cooking. By contrast, Americans spend only four hours on similar chores. The data confirmed that Italians wash the floors in their kitchens and bathrooms four times a week or more, while Americans take on the task only once a week. It's likely that P&G managers rejoiced in this information, knowing they were entering a market where customers are known to use and buy more cleaning materials than the norm.

BLOOM ON GROWTH	*Customer* is the most important word in the vocabulary of business.

So, how could P&G's Swiffer Wet Mop product "flop" in Italy? It did, until the company dug in and began to learn a great deal more than what mere statistics revealed about its Italian customers. As the *Journal* puts it, "What the world's biggest consumer-products companies failed to realize is that what sells products elsewhere—labor-saving convenience—is a big turnoff here. Italian women want products that are tough cleaners, not timesavers. The Italians 'are not ready for convenience in the way Americans are' says Elio Leoni Sceti, chief marketing officer at Reckitt Benckiser PLC, maker of Lysol cleaner and Woolite laundry detergent. 'It's perceived as a step back.'"

BLOOM ON GROWTH   It's not enough to define your customer as a market statistic—you can't get to know a statistic.

P&G eventually came to realize that if it was to succeed in Italy, its products would have to be experienced as get-the-job-done cleaning materials rather than as labor-saving devices.

P&G, one of the best marketers on the planet, got it. Learning that the Italian customers had been using the product to polish rather than mop, as they didn't believe it could handle the tougher mopping job, P&G introduced a product with beeswax for polishing, which was successful. It also introduced the Swiffer Duster, which did a light job well without offering timesaving "convenience"; the product became a huge bestseller in Italy. "Italy," the *Wall Street Journal* tells us, "is now the biggest European market for Swiffer."

This story underscores two vitally important lessons about *core customers*. First and most obvious, what works in one market or with one customer does not necessarily work with others. One size does not fit all—a well-known fact, but one that's frequently overlooked. Second and even more important: it's not enough to define your customer as a market statistic—you can't get to know a statistic.

Go Well Beyond Demographics

Many managers and owners of businesses large and small, when asked to describe their customers, tend to rely on a statistic like "my customers are females 25 to 40 years old" or "my customers are purchasing agents in big industrial companies." You can't get to know a group of people like "females 25 to 40" or "purchasing agents." That's why you must think of your customer or potential customer in the singular—as one living and breathing person. That person you can get to know, and you can develop a close relationship with him or her.

Knowing your customer—fully understanding his or her needs, preferences, and prejudices—is vital to creating a robust and effective growth strategy for your business. Quite simply, you'll have a much better chance of selling your product or service to someone you know and understand.

Stanley Marcus knew that. The brilliant, urbane founder of Neiman Marcus was also the company's visionary and merchant prince. Above all, Stanley was an absolute master in the art of knowing and understanding customers. He knew almost all of his wealthy Texas customers and well-heeled Dallas visitors by first name. He had a close relationship with many of them. Stanley would magically appear in his store "just to say hello," when the famous and not-so-famous customers were trying on mink coats, considering buying diamond brooches, or shopping for expensive gifts "for a friend." Stanley knew what his customers preferred and understood their aspirations. He built a store environment, created a merchandising philosophy, and cultivated a worldwide reputation with those customers' needs and desires in mind. He did this in many obvious and not so obvious ways.

Prior to Neiman Marcus's U.S. expansion, Stanley had only the one store in downtown Dallas at the corner of Main and Ervay streets. Today, this grand old building remains a showcase of fashion for people from all over the globe. When I was a young cub learning the business, I met with Stanley at this store to get his approval of a special print ad that, as in most retail ads, had the store's address just below the logo. Like all intuitive marketers, Stanley not only knew his customers, he also knew what he wanted his customers to think and feel about his brand. Pointing to the address in the ad, he said, "Bob, please remove the address." He added, quite gently, "when you are Neiman Marcus, you don't need an address."

This was a very valuable lesson, and "Mr. Stanley," as everyone called him, was a great teacher. By excluding the address in his ad, Stanley was adding exclusivity to his brand. He was not inviting just anyone into his store, he was whispering to his valued customers, "of course, *you* know where we are located and *you* are welcome." He was subtly giving his customers permission to feel a bit elitist in matters of taste and style. He showed me the importance of knowing your customers and knowing what you want them to think as well as feel about your reputation.

Form an Intimate Image of Your Customer

Obviously, the best way to know the person you're selling to is to sit across from him or her in the quiet of an office or in a corner of your store or across a lunch table. You can learn how she really feels about the new product that you're launching. You can get a sense of his tastes and values by seeing what he orders for lunch or observing the kind of car he's driving. You can hear her talk about her favorite commercial on the Super Bowl. And when the customer feels really comfortable with you, she may talk about her plans to diversify her firm's portfolio of services or he may share his views of your business offering. If you are lucky, you might even get an earful about your prime competitor.

> **BLOOM ON GROWTH**
>
> I've found it quite helpful to form a mental picture of the customer I'm trying to sell to.

When you get well beyond the customer's demographics, you'll understand her or his habits, needs, and goals. Then and only then, you can define your *target customer* in human terms and determine how best to grow your business with him or her.

But what if it's impractical or impossible to meet your customer because he or she is in Hong Kong, Moscow, Boise, or Cape Town? I've found it quite helpful to form a mental picture of the customer I'm trying to sell to, whether or not I can actually sit across the table from the person.

The virtual person in my head may be standing in a supermarket aisle looking at the shelf that displays my products right beside my competitors'. Or, my virtual customer may be sitting in front of a computer in Tokyo studying the design of the new software I e-mailed him. I always look (metaphorically) into my customer's eyes and formulate virtual questions. "How long have you been in the position with your firm? Can you really make this decision or are you just the gatekeeper? What are your company's goals? From which of my competitors are you considering buying? How will you react to my latest price increase? What specific action can I take to persuade you to sign the contract today?" To get to know your customer even better, you might ask that virtual person in your head some personal questions such as "How many kids do you have? What kind of clothes do you wear? What kind of car do you drive?" Getting to know your customer by thinking about her or him in human terms—not as a statistic—will help facilitate a positive sales outcome.

> **BLOOM ON GROWTH** Getting to know your customer by thinking about her or him in human terms–not as a statistic–will help facilitate a positive sales outcome.

Your Core Customer—WHO

In the language of the Growth Discovery Process, your *core customer* becomes your **WHO**. This brief vivid description of the person who can fuel your growth is the starting point in the discovery of your Inside Advantage. Think of your **WHO** as *the core customer most likely to buy your product or service in the quantity required for optimal profit.* Finding ways to grow the business is completely dependent on carefully and precisely defining this potential customer who can drive your sales increase.

Throughout the book, I'll go into detail about every stage of the Growth Discovery Process, showing you how to develop your Inside Advantage and put it to use for growth. But for the purpose of fully understanding the importance of solidifying who your **WHO** is, let's take a minute to review the function of **WHO** and its relationship to **WHAT**, **HOW**, and **OWN IT!**, leading to an Inside Advantage that will jump-start the growth of your business:

WHO + WHAT + HOW + OWN IT! = INSIDE ADVANTAGE

WHO is the *core customer* most likely to buy your product or service in the quantity required for optimal profit.

WHAT is the *uncommon offering* that your business will own and leverage.

HOW is the *persuasive strategy* that will convince your *core customer* to buy your *uncommon offering* versus all competitive offerings.

OWN IT! is the series of *imaginative acts* that will celebrate your *uncommon offering* and make it well known to your *core customer*.

When you have completed all four steps in the process and are engaged in *imaginative acts*, you are fully exploiting your Inside Advantage.

WHO Statements Are the Starting Point for Growth

The way you define your **WHO** is absolutely critical for the future of your enterprise. You've got to do it right, in a forward-looking and unambiguous way.

Let's look at how a business in China realized its growth objective by defining **WHO** in a particularly ambitious way.

According to the *International Herald Tribune*, the Golf Research Group conducted a study of 1,200 golf courses in the United States that found that golf developments with small golf course operations are usually the most profitable to build. As the article points out, however, size matters in China. The golf development of Mission Hills, in Shenzhen, China, half an hour from Hong Kong, is the home to some of the richest people in the world. And it is big, very big. Mission Hills developer Ken Chu and father David Chu had a clear vision of their **WHO** that was in direct contrast to the study and the experience of most golf community developers. The Chus created Mission Hills especially for wealthy customers. In this community they built everything on a grand scale, including 10 golf courses designed by some of the greatest golfers in the game, such as Greg Norman, Jack Nicklaus, and Vijay Singh. According to the article, the Chus constructed homes as large as 9,300 square feet and built 51 tennis courts in the development. The Chus' insight into their customer is keen, as Ken is quoted as saying, "This wasn't just about golf . . . it was about building a community."

 BLOOM ON GROWTH Knowing your target customers and communicating a consistent message to them is a key to growth.

Defining **WHO** in a too-small way might have doomed Mission Hills. Instead, Mission Hills became a high-prestige destination for Hong Kong businesspeople and their guests from all over the world to entertain and socialize. The article notes that grandeur has always been a part of the Chinese tradition, and Chu understood that large, lavish, richly appointed homes, built in a community of mammoth scale, would appeal to his customers, The fact that "all the homes were sold before construction began" certainly validates the importance of knowing and understanding your **WHO**.

It's vitally important to make a strong connection between your **WHO**—your *core customer*—and your **WHAT**—your *uncommon offering*. After all, what we're talking about here is selling your **WHAT** to your **WHO**. But I'll show you how to do that in Part 2 of the book. For now, let's continue to focus on your *core customer*.

BMW, a client I have worked with for years, achieved incredible success in the luxury automotive segment because it remained focused like a laser beam on its *core customer*. At Publicis we worked with almost all the BMW dealer groups in the United States, and no one knows customers better than dealers. As you'll see in the story below, the benefits of knowing your target customers and communicating a consistent message to them is a key to growth.

As we saw in the Stanley Marcus example, it's imperative to get beyond the demographics and instead focus on knowing your customers and recognizing what you want those customers to think and feel.

In one of our many meetings with senior BMW officials, a newcomer to our agency's BMW team proposed an ad that targeted "status seekers," a concept that's all too commonly associated with automotive marketing. Right away, I could see trouble coming. The top German executive immediately stood up and said very sternly, "Excuse me, we do not market BMW to 'status seekers.' We market to drivers who seek the BMW Driving Experience." With just a hint of smile, he quickly added, "Of course, if someone comes into a dealer seeking 'status,' we will not pass up the sale."

"Driving Experience" in BMW's lexicon means the incredibly smooth road handling at high speeds and the quiet growl of the powerful BMW engine. This differentiating concept sets BMW's automotive products and brand apart from the so-called status brands (and all their lower-price imitators). "Driving Experience" is also reflected in BMW's memorable tagline: "BMW—The Ultimate Driving Machine." The BMW executive who corrected my young employee showed how seriously the company took the wants and needs of its customers, and how well it understood what was expected of its automobiles. If asked, he certainly would have defined BMW's **WHO** as people who want to drive and be seen driving the greatest performance car on the road. The automotive category's "intensive care unit" is filled with brands that failed to identify **WHO** in a precise and insightful way.

Contrast BMW's customer focus and marketplace success with Ford Motor Company and its massive bottom-line losses. Ford failed to respond to its customers' evolving wants and needs. It failed to understand that its traditional, loyal American customer was rapidly becoming more affluent and sophisticated. Unlike their parents, this generation of Americans wanted to look and feel different from their neighbors; they were no longer satisfied with a Ford in their driveway; they wanted something more. The customers that Ford had always owned found what they were looking for, and it wasn't in the Ford dealer's showroom. They fell in love with the style, comfort, features, driving experience, and exclusivity of brands like BMW, Mercedes, Infiniti, Lexus, Audi, and, of course, Toyota, which has become the world's largest automaker.

Instead of looking *inside* its business for ways to retain the loyalty of its **WHO** by enhancing the quality and imagery of its well-established Ford, Mercury, and Lincoln brands, this venerable automaker decided to buy growth and borrow imagery.

Ford tried to buy growth with ongoing price promotions to move its once highly respected brands. This price-driven strategy further devalued the imagery of its brands: Ford's once-loyal customers were now faced with having a "cheap" Ford in their driveway.

Then Ford decided to borrow imagery. It acquired Jaguar, Land Rover, Aston Martin, and Volvo. Each of these brands had carefully cultivated an image and built a loyal following, but all needed a substantial investment to grow beyond their particular niche. Given Ford's precipitous sales decline, this was an investment that the automaker could ill afford.

The lessons from Ford's experience are fourfold:

1. You must understand the wants and needs of your *core customer*—your **WHO**.

2. You have to recognize that customers' aspirations evolve, often quite rapidly.

3. You can buy growth, but you can't borrow imagery.

4. Most important, look inside your business for your Inside Advantage.

Whether you are doing business in the United States, Asia, or any other part of the world, *customer* in any language really is the most important word in the vocabulary of business. Customers' requirements, preferences, and prejudices drive *all* product and service purchasing decisions. That's why you must begin the creation of your growth strategy with a precise definition of your *core customer*. Getting **WHO** right is vital.

Don't Let Your Customers Leave You Behind

It's worth noting that customers' needs and desires evolve much more rapidly than most businesspeople perceive. Ford executives were certainly left in the dust by their customers' changing attitudes. In developing countries, these shifts can be both monumental and abrupt. A close look at the dairy products industry in Asia dramatizes this reality. In Japan, China, and Korea, nations that previously consumed very little dairy, people have been developing a huge appetite for milk and yogurt products. According to the *Wall Street Journal*, there is now an enormous demand for dairy products in China as people hear about their health and nutritional benefits, and Mengniu Milk, a major dairy products company, is in the lead in this market, knowing and benefiting from the fact that the market itself is changing. The country's population is exploding, people have more interest in and access to dairy products, and they are becoming even more sports-obsessed in anticipation of the 2008 Beijing Summer Olympics.

This aggressive dairy giant seems intent on capturing a big piece of this market, and of course it is aided by its insights into the new aspirations of the potential customer, including the strong interest in Western-style sports. According to the *Wall Street Journal*, Mengniu Milk recently announced a major deal with the National Basketball Association (NBA) that allows the company to promote its products during NBA games being broadcast in China. In addition, Mengniu is now in a joint venture with the largest yogurt maker in the world, Danone SA, of France.

> Customers' needs and desires evolve much more rapidly than most businesspeople perceive.

If you want to cash in on the booming Chinese dairy market, you'd better understand China's complex cultural and political barriers and realize that your **WHO** is undergoing a sea change.

Juicy Juice—Who's the Customer?

If you have any lingering doubt about the critical role that targeting the correct customer plays in marketplace success, take a look at how my agency grew an unknown juice brand into today's number one kids' juice drink after discovering its real *core customer* and then uncovering its true *uncommon offering*.

When Nestlé acquired the then-tiny Juicy Juice product 20 years ago, the category was filled with popular so-called juice drinks that in reality contained a little juice and a lot of water, coloring, flavoring, and sugar. Kids loved the stuff. But Juicy Juice was different—it contained 100 percent juice with absolutely no added ingredients like sugar and coloring. Without understanding that it had an Inside Advantage to exploit, the company initially marketed Juicy Juice to kids just as though it were like every other juice drink out there: it was sweet, it tasted great, and it was fun to drink. It didn't work. The kids yawned because the liquid they were drinking tasted just fine to them, so moms continued to purchase those ordinary juice drink brands. The result for Juicy Juice was no results, and the product just couldn't get off the ground.

My agency was assigned the brand with the mandate to grow it, and we took a different approach. We observed an important trend: more and more moms were waking up to the need for their kids to consume far less sugar as well as less flavor and coloring additives. So, thanks to the smart thinking of my longtime colleague, Paul MacMahon, we completely redefined the Juicy Juice *core customer*—changing it from a child to his mother because of her growing concern about natural ingredients. Instead of a youngster, the brand's **WHO** became *a mom who wants her young children to get more nutrition*.

As you'll see in Part 2, the shift opened up a whole new growth opportunity, allowing us to redefine the *uncommon offering*—the brand's **WHAT**. The new Juicy Juice **WHO** and **WHAT** made beverage marketing history. We identified and leveraged an Inside Advantage that catapulted Nestlé Juicy Juice into the number one brand position in its category, with sales estimated to be in excess of $400 million per year.

Now that I have proved to you how essential it is to define your **WHO** accurately and meaningfully, let's move our focus to a subject that is central to all of us engaged in commerce: where to look for the *new* customers who will help us grow our businesses.

CHAPTER 2

All Customers Are Not Created Equal

Growth demands that you attract new customers to your business. However, chasing too many new customers or the wrong new customers can end up hurting your bottom line. Identifying, pursuing, and capturing the right customers, on the other hand, will drive both top-line and bottom-line growth. In short, you want a specific customer segment that's substantial enough in size to deliver sales in the quantity required for optimum profit. This *core customer* is your **WHO**. Securing the right *core customers* can open up all sorts of opportunities, unlock a product's true potential, and change the fortunes of a business. The example that follows vividly demonstrates this principle.

When my agency was assigned the Triaminic brand of cold products, we were told that the customer consisted of "the whole family." This assumption was based on the company's own research. It had found that while young children accounted for most of the brand's usage, adults and older children also used the products often. Undoubtedly, the researchers thought they had helped the brand enormously by framing the *core target audience* in the broadest possible terms and thus expanding the potential market for this popular over-the-counter drug. Nothing could be further from the truth.

> Securing the right *core customers* can open up all sorts of opportunities, unlock a product's true potential, and change the fortunes of a business.

When we drilled into the research, we discovered that Triaminic was purchased almost exclusively by a mom for her young children. It appeared to us that other members of the family used Triaminic when they came down with a cold or cough *only* because the medicine was immediately available in the family's medicine cabinet. Learning this, and with the client's agreement, we redefined Triaminic's *core customer* as follows:

WHO: *A mom with young children*

This change proved to be invaluable because the brand could find far more efficient ways to target the narrower, but still very sizable, "mom with young children" customer. More important, our new insight into the real identity of the customer for the product gave us enormous opportunities to dramatize the product's tangible and emotional benefits to this customer, unlock the brand's *uncommon offering*, and develop a highly effective growth strategy around it. We'll continue the story in Part 2, when we examine the idea of *uncommon offering*—the **WHAT** of our Growth Discovery Process. But for now let me leave you with this teaser . . . as we began to discern the medicine's *uncommon offering*, we eventually modified the *core customer* definition yet again, this time to

WHO: *A mom concerned about the dangers of overdosing her young children who have colds*

This illustrates a valuable lesson—as you are defining all components of the Growth Discovery Process, you should consider the wording a work in progress rather than a permanent expression. Refinements, on occasion even wholesale changes, may be required as you learn more or proceed in the construction of your growth strategy. But remember, the goal is getting the **WHO** clear and right, not complex and long.

You may have noticed that the customer target for both Juicy Juice in the previous chapter and Triaminic is *a mom with young children*. However, Juicy Juice targets *a mom who wants her young children to get more nutrition*, while Triaminic targets *a mom concerned about the dangers of overdosing her young children who have colds*. This contrast in the definition of the same fundamental customer target—*a mom with young children*—brings home the idea discussed in the earlier chapter: the necessity to go way beyond a conventional demographic definition of the *core customer*. Relying on a bland, generalized, statistically oriented definition such *as a mom of a certain age and income living in a certain geographic area* would not have delivered a meaningful, actionable **WHO** for either Juicy Juice or Triaminic. *To grow your business, get to know your potential customer well enough to define your **WHO** as an individual with special needs, concerns, and desires.* That's how to motivate your *core customer* to buy your product or service and perhaps even to become your most loyal and valuable customer.

New Customers Look Like Old Customers

What does your most valuable customer look like? Probably a lot like your other customers because your loyal customer is *particularly attracted* to your product or service offering. Figuring out why this customer is so loyal and so committed to buying a lot from you will prove valuable because the easiest and most profitable growth will be achieved by adding additional customers *very much like* your current most valuable customer.

Just who is this "most valuable" customer? Every business would and should define this individual differently because what's "most valuable" to one firm is not to another. Your most valuable customer could be the one who's been with your firm the longest, or the one who delivers you the most profit, or the one who causes you the least hassle, or the one who under any negative circumstance will be the most loyal, or the one who brags about your product or service all the time, or, of course, your most valuable customer could simply be your biggest customer. However, you define "most valuable," this is the type of customer that you want to get because he or she has a strong affinity to your firm. And, here's the good news, there are more of them out there *very much like* or *similar* to him or her.

BLOOM ON GROWTH	The easiest and most profitable growth will be achieved by adding additional customers *very much like* your current most valuable customer.

Your most valuable customer is particularly attracted to your product or service offering. It's probable that new customers very much like this valuable customer will also become well-satisfied customers of your firm. Case in point—BMW introduced the lower-priced BMW 3 Series, the X3 and X5 sports utility vehicles, the very different Mini, and the super-premium Rolls-Royce to attract new customers very much like its current customers. These customer targets are the typical BMW customer in that they are up-market, can afford a luxury car, and they desire the BMW "Ultimate Driving Experience." They differ only in their preference for a particular style and the amount of money they choose to spend for the car they aspire to drive. Did BMW's focus on customers very much like its current customers pay off? Well, last year BMW posted record sales. A growth strategy very much like BMW's will likely generate profitable growth for your company as well.

Gap Designs for the Wrong New Customer

Two recent efforts by large companies provide an instructive example of starkly contrasting strategies to secure new customers. Gap clothing chain's recent makeover didn't work, as the one-time trendsetter attempted to reach for the largest possible mass audience by migrating from the panache and style statements it used to be noted for. *BusinessWeek* reported a great number of company missteps, including limiting the variety and style of fabrics available for the jeans, attempting to make t-shirts trendy again, and pushing black pants via Audrey Hepburn commercials. Gap lost its fashion edge, and customers stayed away in droves. As industry executive Paul R. Charron said about Gap's failed effort, "If you stand for everything in fashion today, you stand for nothing." I couldn't have said it better myself.

Gap has a new president now, Marka Hansen. According to the *Wall Street Journal*: "Ms. Hansen said the Gap brand had defined its customer as 18 to 35 years old, an overly broad target that confused designers and merchants within the company and didn't fit today's niche-focused marketplace. . . . 'While we haven't landed on a specific target today, we will narrow within the 18-to-35 range, and it clearly will not be the 18-year-old,' Ms. Hansen said."

The issue underscores the critical need to define your *core customer* carefully. But Gap executives need to get beyond the demographics. They, their designers, and their merchants must work together to define a truly meaningful *core customer* for whom they can identify, develop, and deliver tangible and emotional benefits.

Starbucks Brews (and Cooks) for the Right Customer

On the other hand, Starbucks recently announced that it would reformulate the recipes of its baked goods to attract and keep health-conscious customers—a rapidly growing group of new customers—who are in every other way like Starbucks' current primary customers. The typical Starbucks customer heads there for a great cup of coffee with the special ingredients he or she wants and, more likely than not, a tasty snack to go with it. But, health-conscious customers might have to go elsewhere for the healthy snack they seek. So, Starbucks is looking inside its business to create profitable growth and is casting a small, precisely positioned net for that health-conscious individual. The lesson once again—all customers are not created equal.

Look for New Customers in Logical Places

To secure other customers *very much like* your most valuable customer, go after customers who now trade exclusively with your closest direct competitors. Your current product or service offering will appeal to them because it's possible that they are very much like your most valuable customer. These new potential customers may be readily identified by location such as address, phone number, or e-mail address, or you may be able to identify them by demographic characteristics such as age, ethnicity, gender, and psychographic characteristics such as sharing an interest in the same intellectual, artistic, religious, or recreational pastimes. They are the low-hanging fruit ready for you to pick. Your current product or service offering will appeal to this fat target without a radical remake or significant additional investment—that's where you gain the bottom-line benefit.

To grow your business, you can also look for customers similar to your most valuable customer. What do I mean by *similar*? The following are a few examples.

Perhaps a current customer similar to your best customer is buying a small amount of products or services from you but is doing most of his buying from your competitor. Reversing this share of market is your job number one.

Another similar potential customer is one in a similar occupation, residential area, or organization closely aligned with your most valuable customer. Here's what I mean: if your most valuable customers are accountants who buy systems from your firm, you might find that other service industry providers such as architects, lawyers, and public relations agencies could also benefit from systems that you can inexpensively modify for their profession. Or, if your most valuable customer brings her clothes to your tailor shop, someone who lives in her neighborhood or her apartment building will probably find your store similarly convenient and your prices affordable.

Other potential customers similar to your best customer who can be transformed into loyal, profitable customers for your firm might also be younger (or older) than your current most valuable customer, bigger (or smaller) in purchasing volume, more (or less) specialized, or located a little farther (or closer) to your business.

Your similar customers can be found with a little bit of work. You can identify these potential customers who are very close at hand with some investigation, ingenuity, brainstorming, determination, and a great deal of digging into dusty customer records, college and high school yearbooks, country club membership rosters, industry trade journals, local newspaper articles, and the like. The total effort will be well worth it, because you can usually find potential customers similar to your most valuable customer.

Match.com recently found a way to stop its slide in subscribers by looking for new customers in all the right places—similar to but older than current customers. With 1.3 million members, it has now grown into the largest online dating site in the United States, according to the *Wall Street Journal*. Instead of competing head on with other sites for the young dating crowd, the *Wall Street Journal* notes, Match.com targeted singles who were 50-plus years of age. It also adjusted its gender targets and even its location targets by looking to divorced women and to suburbanites. It made a modest and economical change in its offering by making the site easier to navigate and more appealing to this new, older customer. It communicated that it was the destination for mainstream daters who want to find dates with similar tastes and desire serious relationships. Gender plays like Match.com's are worth exploring further.

Hugging Men—Hugging Women

This may sound odd at first, but your *similar* customers may merely be of a different gender. If your current customer is female, perhaps your incremental new target customer is her husband and men like her husband. Or if your current customer is male, his wife or women like his wife might well be your new customers. Clearly there are differences in the kinds of products and services that appeal to men and women, but you will find, as in the following example, that the similarities are powerful enough to drive growth.

BLOOM ON GROWTH

Your current customers can be motivated to refer new clients to you.

One remarkable retailer grew by embracing a target that is similar in every respect to its current *core customer*—an affluent, fashion-conscious, and upwardly mobile person living in the same residential area—except for the gender. My friend, Jack Mitchell, and his family have owned thriving, high-quality men's clothing stores in the upscale Connecticut communities of Westport and Greenwich for a long time. A few years ago, they added fashionable women's clothing and, after this effort proved to be highly successful, they enlarged the women's department, adding accessories and, most recently, jewelry for women. The women's business is now a rapidly growing segment of their business—fast approaching the size of their men's business. Why? They grew their business by adding an audience similar in every way—income, location, style, and tastes—except gender to their current audience.

Your Current Customers Know Your New Customers

Your current customers can be motivated to refer new clients to you—new clients who are likely to be very similar to the current ones. The best way is simply to ask a well-satisfied customer to help you grow your business. Do this in person and at the right time and in the right way without embarrassment or hesitation.

Here's how a simple, "personal" request—even though it's from a large international firm—will generate referrals. When my wife and I go to Italy for the summer, we get our car from Peugeot Open Europe. I recently received a letter from this company thanking me for my business in 2006 and offering me an "exclusive membership in their PRIVILEGE club," and providing me with my personalized membership card. The letter discreetly asks me to refer the company's service to a friend or associate and offers me a choice of three modest travel-related gifts for doing so, adding that it will provide us with a global positioning system (GPS) for our car in 2007 if my referral becomes a customer before the end of the year. Now, if a friend, a colleague, or an acquaintance needs a car for a month or more, I am motivated to suggest that that person contact the firm I use—first, because it has given me excellent service, and second, because that GPS could come in handy when we're trying to find that great new pizza place we've heard about in an Italian village with which we're unfamiliar. Peugeot Open

Europe believes, correctly, that the people I rub elbows with here in the States are similar to me in their wants, needs, and expectations and that they would make good customers.

> Don't make the mistake of thinking that approaching customers for referrals or endorsements is beneath the dignity of your business or your customers.

Other large firms, especially service companies, seek new customers similar to their current customers. We have a friend who is in a senior position at a well-known global full-service financial firm that compels its customer service representatives to become actively involved with prominent cultural organizations. Several times a year this friend invites us to the opening of a new exhibit at the Metropolitan Museum of Art and asks us to bring along some friends who might like to hear a Met curator describe the background of the exhibit and its special features. They know that anyone I bring along will be similar to their current customers and good prospects for their services.

Have Some Coffee, Find a New Customer

You don't always have to engage in a systematized program to secure customers similar to the ones you have. Just ask your customer to join you for a coffee or drink. After a very few minutes of chit-chat about his business or family, say something like, "Bill, it's always pleasant to get together with you, but today I'd like to ask you for a big favor. Let me emphasize that I'll understand if you'd prefer not to say yes. I value your business and our personal relationship and would never do anything to disturb it. With that said, here's the favor: would you be willing to serve as a reference for me in my efforts to expand my business—to get a few more customers as loyal and dedicated to me as you are?" If Bill responds positively, continue: "Here's what I have in mind. I am going after the Jane Powers account and, if you're willing, can I ask Jane to give you a call about our performance for you?" If Bill says yes, thank him and send a nice follow-up e-mail or note.

With this very direct and honest request to the right customer, at the right time and place, you could well get the endorsement you need to expand your business. You'll be blown away by the positive responses you'll receive to appropriate requests for advocacy like this. Don't make the mistake of thinking that approaching customers for referrals or endorsements is beneath the dignity of your business or your customers.

The same methods are constantly used by the rich and famous. They do it better than anyone and are completely comfortable with it. If a Fortune 500 CEO wants to meet the CEO of a firm he or she has never been able to sell, a phone call to a mutual friend will result in a golf outing or a dinner party for that purpose. And it's not just a business tactic. Hollywood tycoons use it for raising money for their political or charitable causes, getting their reliable big-giver friends to bring their own friends along to the fund-raisers. To be sure, it's a different form of advocacy, but the objective is still the same—secure a donor similar to other big donors.

If You Need a Large Number of Prospects

Some businesses need a large number of prospects. One example is real estate. If you lease or sell expensive apartments in a recently constructed residential property, invite the current renters or owners to a well-catered open house—at the right moment thank them for being a part of your community and offer one month's rent or a valuable top-of-the-line appliance or a classy trip to those who provide a lead that closes within a defined time period. These tactics work *if* you have a reservoir of well-satisfied customers and do the asking in the right thoughtful, respectful, and low-key way.

The beauty of attracting these supplementary *very much like* or *similar* customers is that your business may have to evolve its offering a bit, just as Match.com and Jack Mitchell did theirs, but *not reinvent* it. Remember that your mission is *profitable growth*, not growth at any price. This objective is best achieved by expanding the definition of your current *core customer*, not striking out for an entirely new one.

Employees Are Customers Too

On occasion, your customers will be your company's own employees. In certain circumstances they can be so influential in the selling dynamic that they can become *the* prime driver of sales success and growth. Well-trained and well-motivated sales associates, as an example, can be very critical in the sale of expensive or complex items like massive machines, fine jewelry, technical products and services, and real estate, to name just a few. Think of those ever-patient sales associates in Home Depot who provide you with invaluable advice and assistance with your complicated plumbing, electrical, or building tasks. Think of the knowledgeable diamond sales associate at Tiffany's who inspires your trust because he or she takes the time to explain the difference between an emerald cut and a pear-shaped diamond and to demonstrate why one looks better on your hand. Or, the ever-smiling barista at Starbucks who, in mere seconds, can whip up your "vente mocha cooler with whipped soy and just a touch of cranberry" so that you can get out the door before your parking meter runs out of time. These highly influential *employee core customers* can be identified, trained, motivated, and inspired to drive your sales success—or they can be overlooked and neglected, contributing to the failure of your business.

What follows is an illustration of an internal "customer" so valuable and so influential that, if approached correctly, can have a huge impact on the financial success of a company.

Siemens, the giant German industrial conglomerate, is one of the world's most successful and respected firms. A few years ago, it made a decision to confront its lack of prominence in the United States and hired our agency to create an awareness-building campaign in the United States.

We did our homework. We learned about Siemens's immense size and exceptional capabilities. Although we were impressed by the diversity of the company's products and services, we did not fully understand its enormous opportunity in America until a senior client described the full potential with this example: "Siemens can construct a new hospital building and provide all the electrical components, communications equipment, heating and air conditioning, and appliances, as well as many of the complex medical devices." In other words, this giant could do something that only a handful of other companies on earth could do—build and furnish a complete hospital with few if any key subcontractors. This is an achievement that can save a customer time, money, and a lot of frustration. The client added, "Siemens wants to secure many hospital projects like this as well as many other large consolidated construction contracts in the U.S."

BLOOM ON GROWTH

On occasion, your customers will be your company's own employees.

Siemens tasked us to reach and favorably influence all targets that could positively affect its success in the United States—architects, developers, the financial community, and business leaders. Groups like these could have great influence in the choice of a firm like Siemens for important construction projects. Our national TV and print campaign delivered increased awareness for Siemens among all these influential target segments.

But, there was a *core "customer"* who could have an even bigger and more direct influence on the client's return on its marketing investment. In this instance, it was the numerous individual Siemens operating units—the highly successful, semiautonomous divisions of Siemens—that had to be persuaded and motivated to work closely together to secure the big, integrated contracts on which Siemens was bidding. Siemens USA management understood this challenge and worked hard to secure the intense collaboration required. The company's successful track record speaks for itself.

There's some important learning here—energizing an internal "customer" is a neverending task. It must be done well and continuously. To optimize financial results, it must be done in a constructive and positive way that convincingly demonstrates the benefits to the "customers" as well as to the company.

It must also be done in a manner relevant to the nature of the firm's business and, importantly, its operating philosophy. Whether your internal "customer" is a couple of staff members or thousands of employees, these high-priority groups require a sense of shared purpose. Team building, training, motivation, and inspiration are essential to marketplace success. Shared financial incentives may also be valuable. The "bottom line" in this context is the bottom line—when sales results are exceptionally dependent on the collaboration of multiple parts of your enterprise, your primary *core "customer"* is both internal and essential.

You now know that accurately and descriptively defining your *core customer*—external or internal—is absolutely critical to your growth. **WHO** is the foundation on which all other components of the Growth Discovery Process are built. In the next chapter, you'll learn how to zero in on your own *core customer*.

CHAPTER 3

Zero In on Your Core Customer

Over the years I've helped many clients identify and define their *core customer* and now I'd like to help you. We—you and I—are going to look for and determine the essence of the customer you must attract to grow your business. Then we'll create a statement of approximately 10 to 15 carefully chosen, simple, and vivid words that express that essence. That will be your **WHO** statement, the first of four components in the Growth Discovery Process, so we must take exceptional care to get it right.

Recently, the great advertising entrepreneur Maurice Saatchi wrote provocatively on the subject of carefully choosing your words. He believes that our fast-moving, digital, multitasking, new-technology world has created the necessity for a new way of marketing. Nowadays, "companies compete for global ownership of one word in the public mind," said Mr. Saatchi. In fact, Mr. Saatchi believes that "one-word equity" has become "the most priceless asset" your company can own. He cites Google, for example, as owning the word *search*. Apple owns *innovation*. America owns *freedom*. Mr. Saatchi believes that it is now imperative "to reduce the complex to the simple without being simplistic." And he urges his readers to pare down "the paragraph to the sentence and the sentence down to the word" in order to reach the one word that, in effect, says it all.

He's on to something. While we are not writing advertising copy in the Growth Discovery Process, and I don't advocate paring down our statements to one word, I do believe that the statements we create in each component of the process—beginning with **WHO**—must be brief, simple, and clear.

Mark Twain is reputed to have said this about a word: "The difference between a perfect word and a near-perfect word is like the difference between lightning and a lightning bug." The task at hand is to define your **WHO** in a few well-chosen words and to weigh every word. When you're finished, you must understand and believe every word. You must make sure that you have captured the essence of your customer. Like all new tasks, this one will become easier as you get into it. You'll quickly learn how to express yourself in a brief and meaningful way.

> **BLOOM ON GROWTH**
>
> Even company veterans may have a hard time setting down on paper the most accurate and meaningful description of their customers.

To help you with your own **WHO** statement, I am providing you with numerous examples of *core customer* statements developed with and for clients in my consulting practice. These clients and their quest for their Inside Advantage will appear and reappear throughout the book. They include a large golf equipment retailer; a publisher of financial data, news, and other information for professional markets; a technology provider for the communications industry; a renowned symphony orchestra; a prominent wealth management firm; and a sports and entertainment advertising agency. Smaller businesses are also represented: a start-up fitness club, a large high-end jewelry and watch store, and an upscale chain of tanning salons. Along with these, I include a variety of national and global **WHO** illustrations from my advertising career.

It would be a mistake to think that these statements are easily arrived at. They are not. They require thought and analysis. Even company veterans may have a hard time setting down on paper the most accurate and meaningful description of their customers.

In my consulting sessions I act as moderator and guide, moving the group of executive attendees through a series of exercises that helps them hone in on and refine the definition of each component in their Growth Discovery Process. Since you've probably not attended one of my sessions, I think it will be instructive for you to be a fly on the wall at one or more of them, witnessing the process in motion, the discussions that take place, the brainstorming and refining of concepts that occur until we reach consensus on a definition, and then how we eventually articulate that consensus.

To that end, throughout the book, I'll take you behind the scenes of one of my consulting sessions. They typically run for a full day and usually take place away from the company's offices, in a hotel conference room or some other isolated place where the meeting cannot be interrupted and the attendees cannot be summoned from the room to take care of some business. I want the participants to focus exclusively on the work we are doing. I'll put you in the room with the group as we work together, sometimes in harmony and sometimes with difficulty, searching for the company's Inside Advantage.

For our **WHO** statement, we're going to work with a medium-sized business-to-business (B2B) company: a publisher that focuses primarily on serving the insurance sector. Specifically, this company publishes multiple weekly and monthly periodicals, online newsletters, and numerous books and reference guides, and it compiles and sells subscriptions to essential databases. It also conducts well-attended industry conferences for a variety of financial services practitioners such as insurance brokers and agents, financial consultants, actuaries, and banking officials.

This firm was founded in 2003 by a private equity company that asked me to help the new CEO and his freshly recruited key executives to define a robust growth strategy. Jumping ahead with the results—in the ensuing three years, the firm consummated three acquisitions and achieved organic growth that more than doubled its revenue. For my description of the group working session, see "A Bob Bloom Consulting Session—Finding Our **WHO**," which follows.

A BOB BLOOM CONSULTING SESSION

Finding Our WHO

The company selects an isolated space in its building for our session—away from the offices where business is being conducted. The room is cavernous—way too big for the 15 or so participants, but we make it work by setting up in a corner of the room. Attending are the CEO, CFO, and senior managers from throughout the company including editorial (the heart and soul of the operation), finance, IT, distribution, marketing, and sales. Behind me are four large easels I have brought to the meeting, upon which rest large flipcharts, some marking pens of different colors, and masking tape to fix pages ripped from the charts to the walls.

I begin with the rules of the road. No interruptions between breaks, no cell phones or BlackBerry devices, and no stepping in or out. I explain that I will provide the process; moderate; aid the effort to achieve simple, clear expressions; and add value to strategy development. I emphasize that everyone in the room must contribute. I announce that for the duration of this meeting, everyone is equal to everyone else. I appoint each person in the room "chief strategy officer of the day." I also make clear that there will be no ridicule or put-downs for bad ideas, and no recriminations after the meeting. And I assure the group that our session will be fast paced, challenging, and intense but also valuable and fulfilling—and maybe a little fun.

Our goal for the day, as I describe it to the group, is achieving absolute consensus for the growth strategy of the firm. And I underscore the value of consensus—every senior executive of the company will contribute to its creation and have a shared role in accomplishing the growth objective. I emphasize that we will begin with **WHO**—identifying the *core customer*—because it is the driver of the other three components of the Growth Discovery Process.

I start by asking the participants for a few words that describe their customer or potential customer. As usual, there is dead silence (no one ever wants to be the first and risk looking dumb). I repeat my request—maybe more than once—explaining that we need to develop a positive momentum so that the thoughts and the words start flowing and the creative intelligence of the group is engaged. The floodgates open, so much so that I ask that only one person jump in at a time so we can capture each suggestion, word for word, and write it in big letters on the charts. I hear "agents," "all people who sell insurance," "brokers," and "anyone involved with the insurance industry."

When each chart becomes full, I number it and tape it to the wall, at times summoning help from the audience so that I can stay focused on the ideas that are erupting from every part of the room.

Within half an hour or so we have about a dozen charts on the walls, each filled with suggested definitions of customers and potential customers such as "insurance consultants" and "financial advisors." I push for even more and insist that the noncontributors get in the game. As always, some of the freshest suggestions come from the quietest participants. Why? Perhaps they had never been asked for their input or never felt empowered to speak out. The human resources person says, "I always hear you guys say that our readers like to think of themselves as 'experts.'" Perhaps she's been holding back until she feels her suggestion is on target. Whatever the case, everyone is now engaged and helping to fill up several more charts with newborn words or phrases describing the customer: "actuaries" and "insurance company executives."

At this point, the CEO asks a question that almost always comes up: "Can we really get to one 10- to 15-word definition that fits our business? We have so many kinds of customers and so many kinds of products and services." My reply is always the same: "You bet we can. And in the next few minutes we will create a simple, brief, clear statement that meaningfully and accurately describes the firm's *core customer.*" Although I am confident, I know that doubts linger in the room, but we push on.

When we seem to have exhausted all options, I take a marking pen of a different color from the one I have been using to write the words and circle those words or phrases on the charts that the group likes. (They have indicated their preferences by raising their hands whenever I point to a word or phrase that appeals to them.) We eliminate the large quantity of duplicates that always turn up. I then explain that we are not seeking a "laundry list" of customers—we are looking for two or three words that accurately describe their *core customer.* Almost magically, the ordinary and obvious words like *agents, brokers,* and *actuaries* are no longer acceptable to the group.

They are now gravitating toward words and phrases that are more inclusive of their customers such as *insurance practitioners, insurance authorities,* and *insurance specialists.* Some are good, and some are lousy, but I jot them all down. Someone from the back of the room yells "insurance professionals!" He explains why he likes it so much: "Everyone wants to feel he or she is professional—it's not arrogant like 'expert' or 'authority.'" The sales manager chimes in on the topic of insurance professionals, quickly adding, "It describes everyone in the industry from the old veteran to the young beginner who believes he's on the road to being a professional." There's a general affirmation in the room that these two words capture the feeling that today's insurance practitioners want to evoke—the feeling that they are indeed "professional" and not merely salespeople or clerks. More emerges later in the session on this key topic.

It is now the moment in the meeting to underscore that, while these two words are dead on, they are not enough to describe the *core customer*. We're really just at the beginning of understanding who this customer is. We need to go on and describe in a very explicit and expressive way what an "insurance professional" needs, desires, prefers, seeks, wants, or demands from a firm like my client's.

At this point the question that is always asked is: "Are we defining our *current* customer target or the *expanded customer* base we want?" I respond: "We want to define the customer we have now as well as the new customer we'd like to capture in the near term—say, in the next few years. We want one all-inclusive statement that is at once ambitious and achievable."

Now I try to bore in a bit, asking each participant to visualize his or her most valuable customer—to create a mental picture of how this customer is using and benefiting from the firm's data, information, and learning tools. This request prompts a profound discussion of how the firm's customer has been evolving. I learn that the time-honored image of the old "insurance peddler" is no longer valid. Some of us remember him as the guy (yes, he was always a male back then) who arrived on the doorstep of a prospect immediately after a child was born to remind the parents in a solemn, grave voice that "no one lives forever." I discover to my amazement that this nice but not too brilliant guy has given way to a new generation of "insurance professionals." The term shouted out earlier in the session has real meaning. This new professional is a proud, well-educated financial expert who is required to know a customer's entire financial picture, offer the right solutions, and explain complex financial products. I find out that almost everything this person deals with is constantly changing—tax regulations, personal longevity, retirement plans, and options for wealth accumulation—and that these changes are creating an almost unquenchable thirst for data, news, education, and information.

Stimulated by this conversation, the group begins to generate fresh and descriptive words to describe the firm's customer. As usual, I have to remind the group that their **WHO** needs to be true, not imaginary, and that we have to get to about 10 to 15 words. I start writing on the clean charts, moving between words already generated and recorded, and new ideas and suggestions pouring out from the group. Everyone gets into the act. We have real momentum. Someone wisely suggests that we use *financial professional* rather than *insurance professional* because that's really what these professionals want to be known for. The group buys in totally.

We soon complete the task of turning the words into phrases that describe how each customer uses, benefits from, and relies on the firm's products and services: *a financial professional who markets insurance products and services* and *a financial professional who provides expert advice to customers about insurance matters*. Finally, we work together to craft a tightly worded statement that brings smiles all around the room. We crack the code about 90 minutes after the start of the program. All doubts have by now evaporated. Our brief statement, notable for its clarity (more important than the actual word count), defines the customer and potential customer target for all products and services of the firm. We now have identification of the *core customer* that can drive all other components in the growth strategy:

WHO: *A financial professional who provides advice and solutions to clients who want or need to be better informed about insurance*

With pride, the group reads and rereads the statement, commenting on each and every word. Someone suggests an alternate word here or there, but he or she is drowned out by the group in favor of the existing expression. They love *a financial professional* because it captures the aspiration of the customer. They agree that this professional *provides* rather than *delivers* or *sells*. They concur that the product and service this person provides is *advice and solutions* and that *informed about insurance* is comprehensive and all inclusive.

This **WHO** statement is an extraordinary accomplishment for the company for several key reasons. First and foremost, every member of the management team has contributed to its creation and is convinced it's dead on. They've achieved total consensus. Second, everyone in the firm will use the same customer definition, and going forward there will be no variance, vagueness, or confusion. Finally, this simple, clear, brief statement becomes the first step in creating the firm's growth strategy.

There are high-fives everywhere, and we stand up to stretch. I call for a short break and ask that everyone return ready to work in the same collaborative fashion on the most important component of the Growth Discovery Process—**WHAT**—the *uncommon offering* that the business can own and leverage.

Finding Your WHO

I hope that I've convinced you of the power of defining your customer and the importance of this definition for driving growth. Perhaps you're now eager to discover your own business's *core customer*. To aid you in this work I've developed a step-by-step procedure doing just that—creating your **WHO** statement.

I've written it assuming that you are the only person in the room. Why? If you are a head of a division or brand in a large or medium-size company, you will have to lead the effort. Or, if you are an entrepreneur with a small staff or no staff at all, you may be in the room alone (or you may feel you are all alone).

1. Begin by quickly reviewing all of Part 1 to refresh your memory. Make a mental note of or create a file on your computer or mark those sentences, phrases, and paragraphs that you find particularly instructive. List any questions you have. They may be answered by the steps that follow or by the frequently asked questions at the end of each part of the book.

2. This is really important: do *not* start drafting the description of your *core customer* right away. Rather, make a list of *all* the customers who come to mind, not just your favorites, and certainly not those customers you wish you had or can never hope to have. Be sure to include the important customers who now belong exclusively to your largest competitors, as they could be your best targets. List those customers whom you share with competitors, as getting more of these prospects' business may be a lot easier than you think. Spend some time looking at your list and push yourself to generate more options.

3. Create a vivid picture in your head of your most valuable customer and keep this virtual person clearly in mind. Add those potential customers that are *very much like* or *similar* to your current most important customer.

4. Put the list away for a couple of hours or a couple of days while you seek some supplementary ideas from people who know your business. These might include your colleagues, if you're working collaboratively, or a few employees, vendors, advisors, and friends, if you're working alone. The fresh perspective you get from other sources will help you add still more customers and potential customers to your list.

5. Carefully examine your list and circle those targets that best represent your current customers and the potential customers you'd like to recruit in the next few years. Be realistic, but remain ambitious.

6. Focus on your highest priority targets. You're not looking for a laundry list of targets, rather you're defining an individual who is or will become your *core customer*. Describe him or her in two or three fresh words. Avoid the common or generic ways to characterize this person. Settle on the brief description that you like best. It will not be set in concrete. It will, in all likelihood, be refined a little later in your **WHO** process or perhaps even in your **WHAT** process.

7. This is the moment to define your customer in far more than demographic terms — to describe what this person needs, desires, prefers, seeks, wants, or demands from a firm like yours. Don't just list the products or services you offer for sale. Use simple, clear words that express what this individual is looking for in the context of your products and services. Create words that are precise and fresh. Keep paring down the statement by editing out words that are not essential, purposeful, or artful. You want no more than 10 to 15 highly descriptive words that capture your *core customer*.

8. Before moving on, take a close look at the **WHO** statements that follow. These are firms of various sizes and types including B2B, high-tech, retail, not-for-profit, and consumer products. Consider them only as a model. Please don't copy them, because each is specific to its business, just as yours must be. I've not given you statements of the brands and companies that have been clients of my agency, as these are confidential. However, I have provided **WHO** statements that have been created by my consulting clients, without the names of the firms and with some modifications to assure confidentiality.

Please note that each of the statements describes the customer as just one person—not a group.

Use the following **WHO** statements to generate ideas and inspire you to create a brief, accurate, meaningful *core customer* statement for your own business.

Core Customer WHO Statements

A National Chain of Suburban Newspapers

WHO: An active suburban homeowning family that cares about enhancing its quality of life and learning about local products and services that satisfy its needs and wants

A West Coast Golf Products Retailer

WHO: An affluent, avid golfer who constantly seeks a better golfing experience

A Global Technology Provider

WHO: A global business enterprise that seeks the expert advice of a technology provider that understands its business

A Renowned Symphony Orchestra

WHO: A frequent patron of classical music concerts who seeks a more passionate musical experience

An Ultra-High-End Jewelry Store

WHO: An affluent local male or female status seeker who is looking for a fashion statement

A Start-Up Fitness Center

WHO: An adult man or woman who wants and can afford an exceptional personal training experience

A Prominent Wealth Management Firm

WHO: A prospective client with assets of $15+ million to invest plus an intense desire for special services and attention

An Upscale Chain of Tanning Salons

WHO: An image-conscious single woman who wants to look and feel better with little investment in time or money

A Sports and Entertainment Marketing Agency

WHO: A powerful marketer with a big ad budget that demands results-driven sponsorship programs

A Publisher of Insurance Industry Data, News, and Other Information

WHO: A financial professional who provides advice and solutions to clients who want or need to be better informed about insurance

A Not-for-Profit Social Services Organization

WHO: An individual, a family, or a community that is underserved in terms of urgent human needs and lack of resources

---

Examine your **WHO** statement one final time. Make sure that every word is meaningful and necessary. Edit where required for brevity, content, and clarity. Ask yourself: is it as simple and artful as I can make it? And ask yourself the most important question of all: can I grow my business by capturing and retaining this *core customer*? If your answer is an unequivocal yes, you have successfully created the first and most important component of the Growth Discovery Process. Congratulations!

The Inside Advantage FAQ—WHO

If you still have questions, take a look at the following FAQ. Your answers may well be here.

Q: What are the basic "ingredients" of **WHO**?

A: The first "ingredient" in your **WHO** statement is a brief phrase that describes your most valuable customer—one person—in a very clear, vivid, and precise way. Here are some excellent examples from my consulting practice: *a frequent patron of classical music; a powerful marketer with a big ad budget; an image-conscious single woman; an active suburban homeowning family; a global business enterprise; a prospective client with assets of $15+ million to invest.* When you read any of these, a colorful picture of a person pops into your head; you can actually visualize this living and breathing human being.

All **WHO** statements should begin this way. The next "ingredient" in this 10- to 15-word statement describes, in a very explicit and expressive way, what your *core customer* needs, desires, prefers, seeks, wants, or demands from a firm like yours. Examples: *a better golfing experience; expert advice of a technology provider; an exceptional personal training experience; special services and attention.* Of course, the remaining ingredient is the word or words that connect the first ingredient with the second ingredient. These words must be carefully crafted to be specific, logical, and creative.

These connecting words and phrases can be anywhere in the statement so long as they make it better, not just longer. Examples: *avid golfer who constantly seeks; a technology provider that understands its business; who wants and can afford; solutions to clients who want or need.* As you work through the process, bear in mind that this is not a modular cookie-cutter process calling for two cups of sugar, a pint of milk, and a dash of salt. This is a creative process: you are accurately, articulately, and creatively describing a person (customer). You're working on a *finely painted word portrait* of your *core customer*.

Q: You say that 10 to 15 words is the right length for **WHO** and the other three elements in the Growth Discovery Process. How many words is too many?

A: Billboard advertising experts have good advice on this matter—any word over six is too many. It's a warning that most advertisers and agencies disregard at their own peril. Try to keep your statements to fewer than 10 words and use the "outdoor rule" when you write more than 15 words.

Q: I still don't fully get the idea that my **WHO** can be written with both my customer and potential customer in mind. Can you tell me why and how I can do this?

A: Your question is one that challenges many readers and clients. First, you must realize that growth without customer retention is counterproductive. So, your identification of your *core customer* must first and foremost focus on your current customers. Next, you have to grow your firm, or you wouldn't have bought this book. So, your *core customer* must certainly be consistent with the needs and aspirations of your potential customers. This may or may not require some specific reference to your potential customers. Take another look at the ultra-high-end jewelry store **WHO** statement where the *core customer* is described as *an affluent local male or female*. As you will read a little later, this retailer was previously focused on selling expensive watches to men, so his **WHO** needed to explicitly reference "male or female." Contrast this with the **WHO** of the upscale chain of tanning salons whose customer and potential customer is predominately female: *an image-conscious single woman*. Your **WHO** must be both accurate and ambitious—and it can be both with a little work and a lot of artistry.

Q: What do you mean when you say, "particularly attracted to" as in "your *core customer* is particularly attracted to your product or service offering"?

A: "Particularly attracted to" means that there is something about your firm that draws the customer to your firm and keeps him or her as a customer—its way of working, exceptional service, user-friendly technology, unlimited return policy, product design, owner or manager who makes the customer feel welcome, and so on. We all have an affinity to a particular vendor, store, brand, service, contractor, or manufacturer that causes us to be a loyal customer. This "stickiness" will keep us loyal to the firm until it fails to satisfy us or until we try an *uncommon offering* that motivates us to switch our loyalty. That's why you must keep up with the aspirations of your customers and not just with industry trends, as the trends will no longer be trendy when you finally hop aboard them. We'll discuss in Part 2 the very bad idea of using price as the "glue" to retain the customer, but I can't let this moment pass without cautioning you that "lower or lowest price" is the least-adhesive business offering of all.

We're now ready to turn to the all important subject of your business offering—your **WHAT**. By now you are feeling pretty confident about where we are going. You know that companies large and small have benefited from accurately defining their **WHO**—their *core customer*. But there is more to learn about business growth. In Part 2 we take a close look at your business and what you offer to your customers. We discover how the right offering can be turned into your Inside Advantage.

Uncommon Offerings

WHAT Can You Offer Them?

WHAT

CHAPTER 4

What Business Are You *Really* In?

N ow that you know how to identify and define the customer who can drive the growth you need, it's time to turn to the most fundamental of all assumptions about your business:

What business are you in?

Not surprisingly, many managers as well as owners of businesses, small and large, when asked to describe their business, tend to focus on the product or service they make or sell: "We make jet engines." "My division sells software to the gaming industry." "I just bought a franchise business and sell ice cream." "We're one of the largest accounting firms in the Northeast." "I manufacture and market a wide line of metal fittings." "We run a chain of family-style restaurants."

Such responses are natural enough, but they are not the right answers to this profoundly important question. Here's why: they only describe the narrow transaction between your business and your customers and that most certainly is *not* "the business you're in." Thinking of a business merely as a commercial transaction is narrow, limiting, and ultimately self-defeating.

It does not allow you to consider and act on the all-important role of the customer's *emotional connection* to your business. That connection is critical to your survival and growth—critical to maintaining the loyalty of your customers and attracting new ones.

If you were asked to describe what business L'Oréal is in, you might reply that it's in the cosmetics and hair care business, selling everything from Maybelline Great Lash mascara to Lancôme Paris–Trésor perfume to Garnier Fructis shampoo. But that description misses the point—and misses all understanding of where future growth and profit might be found.

> **BLOOM ON GROWTH**
>
> To grow your business, you need to fully
> understand what you are offering customers
> in terms of the broad experience that you deliver
> to them—not the narrow transaction between
> you and the customer.

L'Oréal, a client I worked with for many years, is an enormously successful global marketer largely because everyone in the company focuses on the importance of the emotional connection with customers. L'Oréal understands that the company is in the business of helping women *look and feel beautiful*. This business philosophy, developed by the firm's founders and championed by their successive management, is at the very heart of the company's prosperity. L'Oréal's senior executives personally assure that each of the company's brands delivers that important benefit and powerful promise to the target customer. The formulation of the products the company develops, the brand image it portrays, and the marketing it creates all have the objective of getting that message across and using it to establish and maintain an emotional connection with female customers.

For example, with Lancôme Paris–Trésor, the chic of "Paris" is in the product name to inspire the customer's confidence, a famous fashion model is in the ads to connect with the consumer's aspirations, and the point of purchase portrays the model as the customer would like to be seen. The perfume is in a graceful sculptured glass container, and an implied promise of looking and feeling beautiful is in all customer communications. These interrelated emotional elements combine perfectly to retain current customers and continually attract new ones.

Clearly, there is a deep and profound difference between "selling perfume" and "helping women look and feel beautiful." It is a difference that customers respond to—a difference that informs every decision, every action at L'Oréal. In the same vein, note the difference between a golf products store that "sells golf clubs and golfing attire" and one that "enables golfers to achieve their personal ambition on the course." Which would you patronize? When shopping for communications hardware and software for your company, would you rather do business with a company that "sells technology products" or one that "assures customers that they will gain operational efficiency and valuable intelligence from the products we create"? In your personal life, if you had a choice between a fitness center on one side of the street that offers "training experts" and one on the other side that promises to deliver its customers "consistent progress toward health and well-being," which would you join? In each case, the business that offers prospective customers meaningful benefits *and* an emotional experience far beyond a simple transaction will prevail over its competition.

BLOOM ON GROWTH

Thinking of a business merely as a commercial transaction is narrow, limiting, and ultimately self-defeating.

The lesson? To grow your business, you need to fully understand what you are offering customers in terms of the broad experience that you deliver to them—not the narrow transaction between you and the customer.

Your Uncommon Offering—WHAT

In the language of the Growth Discovery Process, your offering becomes your **WHAT**, representing both the tangible benefit of your product or service and the emotional experience you will deliver to your customer. Your firm's offering must be formulated as an overarching positive customer experience, as in the examples above, and be incorporated in every aspect of that customer experience. In approaching your business in this way, you'll identify the *uncommon offering* that you will own and leverage for growth. That *uncommon offering*, once revealed, ultimately becomes your Inside Advantage as, later in my process, you begin to take a series of *imaginative acts* to become well known for your offering.

Let's take a minute now to review the way **WHAT** interacts with **WHO**, **HOW**, and **OWN IT!** in the Growth Discovery Process:

WHO + WHAT + HOW + OWN IT! = INSIDE ADVANTAGE

WHO is the *core customer* most likely to buy your product or service in the quantity required for optimal profit.

WHAT is the *uncommon offering* that your business will own and leverage.

HOW is the *persuasive strategy* that will convince your *core customer* to buy your *uncommon offering* versus all competitive offerings.

OWN IT! is the series of *imaginative acts* that will celebrate your *uncommon offering* and make it well known to your *core customer*.

Your **WHAT**—your *uncommon offering*—defines the existing asset in your business that you can own and leverage. That's why **WHAT** is the most important component of the Growth Discovery Process. It must focus on the customer benefits and emotional appeals that give your business an Inside Advantage. It is the centerpiece of your growth strategy.

Why do I call it an *uncommon offering*? I put a lot of stress on the adjective *uncommon* because it is vitally important that your offering be "experienced" by the customer as neither ordinary nor unique. A common offering is a me-too product or service that anyone can offer, allowing you no advantage over competitors, no room to create the kinds of meaningful benefits and emotional experiences that customers desire.

Opening up just another hamburger joint—one without an *uncommon offering*—to compete with McDonald's, Burger King, and all the other hamburger joints is a recipe for disaster. What could possibly entice you to try yet another fast-food hamburger restaurant, especially one that is unfamiliar, that offers nothing special, and that is located across the street from the well-known burger chains? Probably nothing, and that's why another me-too burger place would probably fail.

Yet, there is a way to make the common hamburger experience uncommon, allowing the new hamburger joint to compete with and even outdo the big fast-food firms. In almost every city and town, there's at least one incredibly successful local burger joint that succeeds against the giants because it capitalizes on an *uncommon offering*, one that has both a tangible and emotional customer benefit. If you've ever been to Roaring Fork in Scottsdale, Arizona, you know exactly what I mean. This fantastically popular Western bistro and saloon features the "Big-Ass Burger," a 12-ounce giant stacked with green chilies and bacon, as well as other spirit-of-the-American-West favorites. Roaring Fork is profiting from its Inside Advantage because it has an *uncommon* brand name that shouts Southwestern fun, an *uncommon* rustic décor to match, *uncommon* products such as its outrageously named gigantic burger topped with genuine Southwestern ingredients, and an *uncommon* owner-chef with a welcoming, outgoing personality. If this *uncommon offering* makes you intrigued, hungry, and dissatisfied with the hamburger you're about to have for lunch, you will certainly make Roaring Fork the first stop on your next trip to Arizona.

Now that you know you don't want a common offering, you may be thinking that you need a unique offering. Not the case! A unique offering lacks credibility in this cynical world we live in, and something that is unique can sound so rare that it may be deemed unreliable or unaffordable. Worse, a unique offering may not endure because it can be knocked off overnight at a lower price point or made suddenly obsolete by technology. Instead, you want an offering that is attainable, enduring, and located in that inviting "sweet spot" between common and unique—and that's the highly competitive place I call *uncommon*.

Consider an ordinary tennis racket—it has strings top-to-bottom and side-to-side, but highly competitive tennis players, amateurs as well professionals, consistently win by finding the racket's "sweet spot." As you read on, we'll continue to explore the simple, but profoundly important *uncommon offering* concept because finding the right one for your business will help you discover and exploit your Inside Advantage.

You Already Possess an Uncommon Offering

Hidden in every business, including yours, is an *uncommon offering* waiting to be revealed and turned into an Inside Advantage with a *persuasive strategy* and series of *imaginative acts*. At first, it may appear that an *uncommon offering* does not exist. Believe me, it does! You just need to know how and where to look for it. Your *uncommon offering* will become *the* essential component of your growth strategy.

T.G.I. Friday's, another famous client I worked with at Publicis, is a great example of what I mean. An international franchisor, Friday's was a pioneer in the theme restaurant category. Theme restaurants, which we are all very familiar with now, were developed to provide customers a dining "experience," not just a place to eat food. Today there are theme restaurants in every category — from steak to Italian to Asian — and in just about every city in every part of the globe.

Friday's early success is legendary. But over time its offering, unique at the beginning, was copied by many aggressive new competitors like Applebee's and Chili's. Each new competitor offered a twist on the theme idea and its own enticing tangible benefit. Applebee's offered a more contemporary ambiance, and Chili's offered a flavorful Southwestern cooking style. Friday's suffered.

> **BLOOM ON GROWTH**
>
> Hidden in every business, including yours, is an *uncommon offering* waiting to be revealed and turned into an Inside Advantage with a *persuasive strategy* and series of *imaginative acts.*

When executives of this mature restaurant chain asked us to help them reinvigorate their business, we entered into a discussion with them about the alternative strategic differences that Friday's could exploit to retain and grow its customer base. We considered Friday's colorful turn-of-century décor, bountiful portions, fun bar scene, and attractive special prices. Great stuff, all. But the copycat competition was already bragging about many of these same obvious, tangible attributes. We needed an emotional benefit that Friday's — and only Friday's — could own.

Eventually we discovered it.

Friday's *uncommon offering*—its **WHAT**—was inside the business, staring us right in the face. It was hidden in the T.G.I. Friday's brand name itself: *going to T.G.I. Friday's any day of the week makes you feel like it's the best day of the week—Friday.* For most of us, Friday signals the end of another workweek and the beginning of our time, a time to enjoy life and the rewards of our labor. Celebrating Friday has become a tradition in America and many other parts of the world, and the phrase "TGIF—Thank God It's Friday!" is exclaimed by work-weary people everywhere as they crowd into bars and restaurants to kick off the weekend.

With TGIF as its brand, Friday's and only Friday's could invite customers to have their celebratory experience on any day of the week because every day is TGIF inside its restaurants. In other words, its very name, unlike any competitor's brand name, beckons customers inside their nearby Friday's to experience the fun and excitement of an end-of-the-week party. And a party atmosphere prevails inside each Friday's restaurant. Smiling bartenders clang bells and waitpersons emerge from the kitchens with platter after platter of piping-hot finger food. The noisy crowd loves all the Friday's action. Tables are always filled with giant portions of fries, burgers, and other hearty orders for fun-loving families, friends, and workmates.

Friday's owns this *uncommon offering* to this day and continues to leverage it. Displayed in giant letters over the doorways of its newest restaurants are the words:

IN HERE, IT'S ALWAYS FRIDAY.

Needless to say, this valuable *uncommon offering* is reflected thematically in the company's public face. Everything the company does, says, and offers is built around its valuable *uncommon offering*, providing the emotional connection that customers want and expect. Print ads, television commercials, and restaurant décor reflect it. Take a look at the Friday's Web site (www.tgifridays.com)

and you'll get a glimpse of what I mean. Items as small as gift cards carry images of a party going on, a celebration that we'd all like to join. Its retail packaged foods are party foods: dips and popcorn chicken. Everywhere you look, the offering is reinforced and the invitation to join the party beckons: "Everyone could use more Friday's."

Isn't that the truth!

Friday's succeeded in transforming its entire customer experience into an "uncommon" reality. At Friday's virtually every customer touch point is informed by its offering, and management has truly turned it into the company's Inside Advantage. This powerful business asset, in combination with recent menu innovations, has enabled the company to maintain its significant share of the U.S. casual dining market in the face of tough competition and expand its operations around the globe. As of May 2007 the firm, according to its Web site, had 884 restaurants in 47 states and 55 countries.

Squandering an Uncommon Offering

Many companies believe that they can patch up the flaws in their offering with dynamic marketing. They are wrong. Colorful ad campaigns and clever slogans are no substitute for the real thing. To have enduring success, you must have an honest and meaningful *uncommon offering*, like T.G.I. Friday's, and make it an integral part of your customer's experience with your product or service. On occasion, I'm asked by a client to "invent" an *uncommon offering*. I always refuse because the effort will surely fail, and quite obviously, it's unethical. Sure, you can deceive customers for a while, but as my dad used to say, "No amount of great advertising can make up for a lousy product."

But what if you have a great product and a great brand, but a serious flaw in your *uncommon offering*—one that's so severe that it's preventing your growth or, worse, is threatening your very existence?

One of the world's most distinguished automobile brands is Alfa Romeo. When a vintage Alfa Spider roars down the street, no one fails to take notice of the car—and, of course, its driver. Alfa Romeo's 96-year racing heritage, stylish Italian hood ornament, powerful engine growl, and rakish design are familiar to anyone who loves elegant performance cars.

What a powerful *uncommon offering*!

> Many companies believe that they can patch up the flaws in their offering with dynamic marketing.
> They are wrong.

A while ago, our New York office was assigned the task of generating increased sales for the Alfa Spider and introducing a new Alfa sedan in the United States. We were excited by this important new assignment, but were soon confronted by an awful reality: Alfa had a terrible reputation for reliability and poor maintenance service in America. Our ads, however effective, could not overcome this serious flaw in the Alfa offering—a flaw so severe that the brand eventually withdrew from the U.S. market.

Painfully, Alfa learned that merely promising a genuine, well-known, and highly appealing *uncommon offering* is not enough; it has to be consistently delivered at every customer touch point, particularly in product maintenance and customer service. How many times have you enjoyed a great meal in a restaurant, but endured such awful service that you never again set foot in that restaurant and then spread the word about your dreadful experience there? That restaurant has far more to do than repair its reputation—it has to permanently fix its flawed service or its door will close permanently.

Here's the good news about Alfa. Fiat, the current owner of Alfa Romeo, recognized this reality. The *Financial Times* recently reported that the company is "overhauling [its] dealer networks and rolling out new models." Fiat's ambitious goal for Alfa is turning the brand around, and the company is "preparing for a planned 2009 launch in the United States, where it has not sold cars since 1995." The company's new focus on reliability and service is critically important to reclaiming Alfa Romeo's enviable reputation for excellence. Remember—to own and leverage your *uncommon offering*, customers must experience its special qualities each and every time they purchase or use it!

There Is No Such Thing as a Commodity

What if you are in a so-called commodity business, where conventional wisdom would say it's impossible to offer customers anything uncommon? Conventional wisdom would be wrong: even the most commonplace product or service can be turned into something special, appealing, and different if you take the time and the effort to identify its *uncommon offering*. Searching for an *uncommon offering* in a commodity product or service is a worthwhile endeavor, as it can transform the company that markets it.

BLOOM ON GROWTH

> Remember—to own and leverage your *uncommon offering*, customers must experience its special qualities each and every time they purchase or use it!

An *uncommon offering* must be kept uncommon by celebrating the customer benefits it delivers at every customer touch point, as Friday's does so well. That's when you *own* your Inside Advantage and that's what **OWN IT!** is all about. Unless you *own* your *uncommon offering*, it can be copied, undercut by cheaper products, or outflanked by products that offer more profit to the so-called middleman such as a distributor, broker, restaurant, or grocery store that sells the product to the ultimate customer. Let's take a close look at how Perrier, bottler of what may be the most famous water in the world, was affected by some of these issues.

Perrier has been bottled at Source Perrier in Vergèze, France, since 1863. The exceptional carbonation found in Perrier comes, as the company likes to say, from "a naturally occurring source found deep beneath the spring." Big bubbles, and lots of them, are Perrier's *uncommon offering.*

You wouldn't be alone if you were to wonder about the notion that consumers would be willing to pay a great deal more for a bottle of water shipped all the way from France, even if they adored big bubbles. People who doubt this phenomenon were and still are wrong.

The agency I acquired in New York was hired to introduce Perrier into the United States. The label on the now-famous green bottle was designed by one of our talented graphic designers. After rejecting many narrow niche positioning options and all the usual soft drink industry clichés, the agency and client decided to capitalize on America's emerging interest in health and fitness. Perrier's refreshing natural effervescence fit perfectly with this health and fitness craze, so it was introduced as a healthy alternative to alcoholic beverages and soft drinks. To celebrate Perrier's image as a healthy alternative, the brand was an early sponsor of the now-famous New York City Marathon. Suddenly, ordering Perrier in restaurants and serving it to guests at home became "chic." Perrier grew like crazy, and the brand became a national success, selling 300 million bottles in 1988.

It's difficult to stay on top (of any heap) forever, even if no disaster strikes. But disaster did strike at Perrier. There was a prolonged product recall, and the restaurants and grocery stores had no healthy "big bubbles" to sell to the many customers clamoring for the then-chic beverage. Almost immediately, the market was flooded with copycats. Unknown brands with "artificial" bubbles abounded, many that delivered far more profit to the middleman (in this instance, the retail trade) than Perrier had provided. Overnight, Perrier was replaced on shelves and tables all over America with second-tier or copycat water products with made-up names. When Perrier returned to the market, it had lost some of its chic and almost all of its distribution space and clout. The agency also lost the business.

Years later, we were once again assigned the Perrier brand. Although the ad budget was far more modest, we created some innovative TV ads that, quite appropriately, celebrated Perrier's special offering—its effervescence. One featured an exotic girl in a shimmering long dress made of sequins that magically turned into floating bubbles. The ads were artistic, but in the face of decreased chic and distribution, the sales needle didn't move enough to satisfy us or our client.

We tried once more to stoke up Perrier's sales by creating one of the funniest radio campaigns ever, featuring the great Orson Welles as the voice. Welles was so versatile that he played multiple characters in every commercial. As Dracula—after sipping blood from a victim, with menacing music in the background, he intones, "It's good, but it's not Perrier." As Lawrence of Arabia, lost in the desert for weeks, he finally finds a well with fresh, cool water. He drinks and utters the same line: "It's good, but it's not Perrier." The ads were arresting, funny, and highly acclaimed, but sales response was insufficient, and the campaign was discontinued.

Although we executed well, the Perrier product recall had invited competitors from every corner of the United States to jump into the vastly expanded bottled water category. The players were far too numerous for any brand, including the first-to-market Perrier, to dominate.

This is not, however, a story about the demise of a great brand. On the contrary, Nestlé took over Perrier in 1992 and formed Nestlé Waters SA, which has become the world's number one marketer of bottled water, with 60 water brands in its portfolio. With

Nestlé's marketing muscle, Perrier is thriving in the United States and around the globe. Today, as always, the natural carbonation found in every bottle of Perrier is exactly as it is at the Vergèze spring. Perrier Sparkling Natural Mineral Water and its all natural lemon and lime products are the beverages of choice for people everywhere who love big bubbles. This is persuasive evidence that there's a lot of money to be made from a product or service with an *uncommon offering.*

Perrier is now using its *uncommon offering* to win an entire new generation of "big bubble" customers in America with a whole range of creative and fun initiatives. We'll look into its *imaginative acts* in Part 4, where we discuss **OWN IT!**

More Ways to Enhance a Commodity

Manufacturers of so-called commodities can keep even the most aggressive competitors at bay when they own and leverage an *uncommon offering*. Here's a convincing example. AES Engineering, based in the United Kingdom, produces common-place engineering seals for complex machines. According to the *Financial Times*, "AES has become as much a consultant as a manufacturer," having made the decision to provide highly customized service for each customer, including specifying the type of seal needed, manufacturing the seals, and then maintaining the seals after installation. By adding this highly valued service component to its business, the company has been able to combat Chinese manufacturers that use low-cost labor to sell equivalent products at cut-rate prices. AES Engineering defended its position in the marketplace and lifted its business out of "commodity" category by creating and capitalizing on an *uncommon offering*.

The creativity with which AES tackled the threat from low-cost competitors will be needed by the "mom-and-pop" retail shops in developing economies all around the world because Wal-Mart and other giant retailers are aggressively seeking international growth. Right now India is facing this huge challenge from the world's largest retailer. According to the *Financial Times*, Wal-Mart has announced a partnership with India's Bharti Enterprises to set up hundreds of stores that will be operated under the Wal-Mart brand. India has been relatively free of any kind of organized retailing until now, a condition that has allowed millions of small shops to flourish throughout the country.

Will all the small shops in India simply disappear under the onslaught of Wal-Mart and the other giant merchants who are sure to follow? Will the Indian customers abandon their small-shop owners for a broader selection of goods at lower prices? Only time will tell, but if what's happened in developed nations around the globe is any indicator, many small Indian shops will perish, while still others will look deep inside their small business for an Inside Advantage that they can use to survive and thrive. These more nimble and creative shop owners will discover their hidden potential, and they will turn their small size into a big customer benefit. They will identify an *uncommon offering*—a specialization they can own. Possibilities include specializing in hard-to-find shoes in big and small sizes, specializing in high-value repair services to extend the life of the home appliances that the store sells, and specializing in hard-to-get expert advice for the complex technical office products that the business sells. Yes, the big opportunity, and perhaps the only opportunity, for the small shops of India is to capitalize on a specialized or customized product or service to attract and retain new customers; they will do this by using their *uncommon offering* to grow their business so as to provide customer benefits the giants can't offer. The small shops of India must come to the realization that you don't have to be bigger or better than your competition— you have to be different.

What's Uncommon about a Screwdriver?

Are wrenches, screwdrivers, or hammers common? Not if they're sold by Barbara K, a company that has been able to create an *uncommon offering* around exactly those types of products targeted exclusively to women. Several years ago, Barbara, a single parent with little tool industry experience, launched a line of great-looking, ergonomically designed tools exclusively for women, who, in rapidly growing numbers are the do-it-yourself experts in their homes and apartments. Barbara K provides this very sizable female customer segment with a tangible benefit (*a well-designed contemporary product engineered to fit comfortably in a woman's hand*) and an emotional benefit (*a way to be at ease with and gain self-confidence from implements traditionally wielded by men*).

Capitalizing on her entrepreneurial drive and her *uncommon offering*, Barbara's specialty tools are now a hot item in Home Depot, Bed Bath & Beyond, and other big chains. Barbara has published two books on tools for women and is a frequent guest on network TV programs like NBC's *Today* show. She has succeeded in making the commonplace uncommon and, additionally, has infused it with her personality. Now Barbara has an even bigger task than launching a promising start-up with an *uncommon offering* — she has to grow her business.

While *uncommon offerings* can indeed be found in commodity products and services and imaginatively exploited, the challenge facing this kind of segmented business is no less daunting than in other businesses: consistently generating profits to invest in growth. Barbara K's future growth can come from numerous carefully planned strategic initiatives such as diversifying its product line, expanding its distribution, or licensing its brand. Whatever strategy is used, Barbara K must realize rapid and profitable growth.

Finding the Uncommon in Exercise

Another business that has found the *uncommon offering* within the commonplace is Curves, the fitness franchiser that has gyms that have sprung up all over the world. This enterprising company, a Publicis client, has achieved exponential growth with its small, inexpensive exercise facilities that cater exclusively to women.

Founders Gary and Diane Heavin—a husband and wife team—opened the first Curves fitness center in 1972. Gary understood the fitness industry, and Diane had a passion for exercise and experience in marketing. Curves was an immediate success because the concept was designed from the ground up to eliminate all the emotional barriers for its very particular *core customer*. Curves has no mirrors, locker rooms, or male customers. Its workout requires only 30 minutes; it's a commonsense, supportive, and inexpensive way for women who may not be in shape to enjoy getting fit. Curves created an uncommon experience by combining a quick-in, quick-out program of strength and cardiovascular training with weight management for women who wanted to avoid the intimidation of a mixed-gender workout experience.

At last count, the company has in excess of 10,000 Curves locations and four million members worldwide. Curves has made the commonplace uncommon by offering its *core customer* a tangible benefit: *fitness* and *weight loss* and an energizing and empowering emotional benefit: "the power to amaze yourself." The brand's *uncommon offering* is celebrated in all of its internal and external communications. Curves' Inside Advantage has enabled it to become the fastest-growing franchisor in the world.

Unique Offerings Are Uniquely Dangerous

Now let's move to the other end of the spectrum of offerings. If common offerings are to be avoided, then developing and owning a "unique" offering must be quite desirable, right?

Sorry—the exact opposite is true.

Unique offerings are just as difficult and challenging as common ones, but for different reasons. Unique offerings cut both ways: they offer unlimited upside potential, but they are also vulnerable to quick, devastating, and expensive failure. Their extreme vulnerability stems from their "perishability"—competitors observe your success and rush into the market, attempting to copy what you are doing or do you one better through technological innovation and lower costs. Both are dangerous threats to any offering, and they frequently combine to hammer businesses into the ground that are founded on unique products.

The truth of this principle is seen in the high-tech graveyards where today's sensation becomes tomorrow's recycling. In the personal computer area the innovations and early successes of companies such as Gateway, Compaq, Atari, and Commodore were soon spoiled by competitors with more unique platforms and deeper pockets.

In more recent years, people thought Yahoo! was pretty unique until Google came along. Now Yahoo! is challenged by this formidable and audacious competitor. Google is flying high by making consistent, massive investments in a stream of innovative products, such as Google Earth, Google Image Search, Google Video, Google Maps, and Gmail. This deliberate strategy of constantly launching exciting new products and services is designed to keep its competitors off balance and in a constant state of catch-up. If this brilliant strategy can be maintained and if Google continues to keep a nanosecond or two ahead of its competitors, it could well defy history, maintaining its leadership and securing its status as the most audacious company that's ever existed. To sustain ownership of a unique offering of any kind, a firm must construct an enormously expensive cost-of-entry barrier and then persistently maintain its lead over the competition.

So only go down that road if you are prepared and properly funded. Think of the infrastructure investment made by eBay,

Amazon.com, Wal-Mart, and FedEx. Only a relentless management team with deep pockets can afford to continuously invest in staying unique. If you're relentless and have access to almost unlimited capital—great! If not, don't bet on always being unique.

Many unique products and services that were first to market have found themselves severely challenged by copycats and aggressive companies with enormous scale and vast financial resources. Thirty years ago, Charles Schwab introduced a truly unique concept: discount brokerage services. This first-to-market alternative to fixed cost, high-priced stock trading is now competing with a plethora of online and offline cut-rate options created by a wide variety of technological advances. Wall Street also reinvented itself to compete head on with Schwab by offering multiple ways for customers to trade at numerous price points. Although Schwab remains a successful company, it has been unable to own and fully leverage the unique concept it invented.

> **BLOOM ON GROWTH**
>
> To sustain ownership of a unique offering of any kind, a firm must construct an enormously expensive cost-of-entry barrier and then persistently maintain its lead over the competition.

Today, price competitors from across the street and across the oceans are a huge challenge to all businesses built on a unique low-cost model. Dell, once an impenetrable low-cost direct-to-consumer fortress, is experiencing margin erosion due to global technology advancements and intense competition from emerging countries in which workers are low paid. In fact, in the view of some people, this great company that turned computers into commodities has found itself commoditized by ambitious competitors who figured out how to copy or improve on Dell's low-cost model. The *Wall Street Journal* put it this way: "buying behavior in the PC world has changed dramatically. . . . Much of the recent growth in

PC demand has come from consumers buying laptop computers at electronics retailers like Circuit City Stores Inc. and Best Buy Co." The *Journal* adds: "Asian rivals like Lenovo Group Ltd. of China and Acer Inc. of Taiwan have gained ground in the global market, and a resurgent Hewlett-Packard Co. recently surpassed Dell to become the world's largest PC maker in terms of units sold, according to some research firms."

In response to the worsening fortunes of the company he founded, Michael Dell relieved CEO Kevin Rollins of command and returned to day-to-day management of the company. His mission is to reenergize the company and recapture the innovative growth strategies of the past. Can he do it? No one should underestimate the drive and the abilities of this great corporate leader. Nor should one underestimate the task he faces.

H&R Block was once the undisputed leader in tax preparation, well known for its offering: easily accessible, inexpensive tax preparation. In fact I would venture to say it "owned" that offering at one time. But today, H&R Block's position has eroded. It faces severe competition from many sources: other tax preparation chains, professional CPA/accounting firms, mom-and-pop providers, Internet products like TurboTax, many nimble online sites, and the Internal Revenue Service itself, which is now encouraging direct online filing. H&R Block failed to transform its model quickly enough to meet the rapidly changing needs of its loyal customers. Instead of investing in its early-to-market offering with a consistent stream of product and service innovations, user-friendly technology advances, and strategic initiatives to cement a strong emotional connection with worried, perplexed, and harried taxpayers, the firm has invested in unrelated services. Even worse, its unrelated mortgage products and investment services offerings have resulted in multiple financial problems.

I am not arguing against innovation or investment in new and unusual products; after all, that's how progress is made in any economic society. Most of us would love to have the success, rewards, and respect that Charles Schwab, Michael Dell, and Henry Bloch have earned. They are all great innovators who deserve their personal success, but they had to make exceptionally heavy and potentially risky investments in what were unique offerings at the time of their introduction. Now, their companies, facing new technologic, economic and global challenges, must reinvest in their once-unique offerings just to remain competitive, let alone unique.

Remember that almost all unique offerings fail. Only very occasionally does a storybook ending occur with a Michael Dell or Charles Schwab becoming highly successful and extremely wealthy. They are the people we hear about in the media, while lost to history are the stories of the hundreds of thousands of corporations that go belly up and entrepreneurs who are forced to close their businesses.

Juicy Juice—What's the Uncommon Offering?

Before you spend your energy and risk huge amounts of capital trying to make your business unique, try my approach: search inside the business for the *uncommon offering* that you can own and leverage and, to assure its vitality and endurance, keep it fresh, contemporary, and relevant. Here's how we did exactly that, growing Nestlé Juicy Juice into today's number one kids' juice drink by discovering an *uncommon offering* the brand could own and leverage.

You'll recall from an earlier chapter that my agency was assigned the task of growing the Juicy Juice business for Nestlé. The brand's previous owners had thought the *core customer* for the juice drink was kids, and they had developed and marketed an ordinary kids-oriented offering for the juice—fun and more fun. That strategy failed. When we took on the account we realized that growth would come not from kids but from their mothers. Moms were becoming increasingly aware of all the sugar and junk in the "juice" drinks their children were consuming. Redefining the *core customer* gave us the opportunity to leverage the then-uncommon product contents: *100 percent pure juice that's healthful for your kids because it contains absolutely no added ingredients.* It's surprising and hard to understand in today's age of hypernutritional awareness that this special asset had gone unrecognized and unexploited. It's fair to say, I think, that Juicy Juice helped to launch the still-evolving consumer awareness of proper nutrition.

We recognized that we could offer the brand's *core customer*—the nutrition-conscious mom—both a *tangible customer benefit* (100 percent natural juice) and an *emotional customer benefit* (it's healthful for your kids!) We used these interconnected customer benefits to construct a powerful **WHAT**. In the language of my Growth Discovery Process, Juicy Juice had an *uncommon offering* it could readily sell to its *core customer*:

WHO: *A mom who wants her young children to get more nutrition*

WHAT: *100 percent pure juice that's healthful for your kids because it contains absolutely no added ingredients*

We were confident that our **WHAT** would be instrumental in the growth of Juicy Juice. We had come a long way toward the formulation of an Inside Advantage. But our work was not done, not by a long shot.

BLOOM ON GROWTH

> Knowing what business you really are in is not as simple as knowing the business transaction you engage in with your customers.

We still had a great deal of work to do—we had to convince moms to buy Juicy Juice instead of the competitors' me-too offerings. Later in the book you'll learn how we crafted this highly competitive *persuasive strategy*. We'll complete the Juicy Juice story toward the end of the book, where you'll see how we developed a series of imaginative initiatives to make the brand well known to moms. As you saw earlier, Nestlé Juicy Juice rocketed into the number one brand position in its category. Knowing what business you really are in is not as simple as knowing the business transaction you engage in with your customers. Yet such knowledge is critical to your growth strategy and to leveraging your Inside Advantage for growth. As you've seen, the business you are in is wrapped up in the tangible and emotional benefits you offer your customers, and both are key to developing your *uncommon offering*.

In the next chapter, we'll spend some time discussing why these tangible and emotional benefits are so interdependent and how they will support and ignite your **WHAT**.

CHAPTER 5

Where Tangible Meets Emotional

Y ou should view your *uncommon offering* as the way your product or service is experienced by your customers, the way it helps them by providing them with tangible benefits and inspires them with positive emotional experiences.

The idea behind a tangible benefit—the way your business helps your customers—is obvious enough. Your business must assist or support the customers in some way—providing them with a product or service they need and value: a gasoline (petrol) station sells fuel to a customer so her car can function; iPod sells a customer a small portable device on which he can easily and cheaply download music and video; a manufacturer of industrial bearings sells a customer devices that significantly reduce friction in her industrial equipment. These are all tangible benefits.

The emotional experience your business evokes in your customers is another thing altogether, and you do evoke emotions—positive ones, I hope—whether you intend to or not: the gasoline you sell to a customer enables her to get to Grandma's house without fear of running dry and becoming stranded on the highway. The free, unasked-for windshield washing you provide as an extra service makes her feel you are taking care of her, making sure she can see the road better at night. An iPod allows the customer to download music legally, without fear of prosecution, and it not only entertains the customer but it also animates him. The whole experience enriches the customer's life. A manufacturer's bearings allow or inspire its customer to design industrial equipment that operates longer, more quietly, and with greater fuel efficiency, thereby raising productivity and possibly profits. As you see, your customer always has some kind of experience—good or bad—whenever he or she comes in contact with your business, products, or services. Here's the point: you can deliberately influence your customer's entire experience with your firm, or you can simply let it happen.

I want to encourage you to create an *uncommon offering* that will consistently and positively shape your customer's total experience with your company. This action, more than any other, will help your business grow. That's why your *uncommon offering*—your **WHAT**—is the most important component in the Growth Discovery Process.

> **BLOOM ON GROWTH**
>
> You can deliberately influence your customer's entire experience with your firm, or you can simply let it happen.

What your customers feel and experience at the hands of your company is your *uncommon offering* from their perspective. Your highest business priority is to consistently provide a total customer experience that will positively influence each customer's perspective about purchasing products and services from your firm.

As you've seen, the tangible customer benefit—what you do to help each and every customer—is only one part of the customer experience. The emotional customer benefit—what you do to inspire the customer—is the other part. These dual benefits are interrelated; to drive your growth, both benefits must work together in complete harmony. Your product or service must help your customer throughout the purchase and usage cycle. And, you must inspire your customer throughout this cycle as well.

What can you do to inspire a customer? Inspire her to feel confident that your switching device will perform the required function efficiently, effectively, and with minimum maintenance. Inspire him to be proud to ride the motorcycle he purchased from you. Inspire him to feel well dressed in the blazer he carefully selected at your store. Inspire her to feel that she can rely on the legal counsel she received from you. Inspire her to feel excited about taking her dad to your restaurant for his birthday.

> **BLOOM ON GROWTH**
>
> Your product or service must help your customer throughout the purchase and usage cycle.

The goal is to inspire every customer to want to be your customer time after time after time. That's why your *uncommon offering* must be genuine, true to the customer's actual experience, and consistently delivered day in and day out.

What follows are some examples of *uncommon offerings* powered by interrelated tangible and emotional benefits.

The Right Medicine for the Right Illness

In an earlier chapter we discovered that Triaminic was purchased almost exclusively by a mom for her young children. We also found out that other members of the family used Triaminic when they came down with a cold or cough *only* because it was immediately available in the family's medicine cabinet. Learning this, and with the client's agreement, we redefined Triaminic's *core customer* as follows:

WHO: A *mom concerned about the dangers of overdosing her young children who have colds*

The redefinition of Triaminic's *core customer* had a tremendous impact on reshaping its **WHAT**. To create an *uncommon offering*, we looked deep inside Triaminic's business from the perspective of a mom with children under the age of 10.

To learn more about the ways the medicine helped the customer, we studied its ingredients, packaging, labeling, and so on. We searched for distinguishing characteristics—existing tangible benefits that were real and true to the brand. We found that each of Triaminic's products was symptom-specific—one product had ingredients for fever, another had ingredients for coughs, still another had ingredients for sniffles, and several others had different sets of ingredients, as well.

But here's the astonishing piece of data that would have a profound effect on the formation of Triaminic's *uncommon offering*: one of our research professionals, while digging through piles of recent as well as old research, found that, unlike her own mom, moms of this generation were self-diagnosing and treating their kids' minor illnesses. Why? They were taking up the chore themselves because most medical insurance plans no longer covered pediatricians' involvement with so-called minor illnesses. Moms could no longer whisk their kids to the doctor at the first sign of a cold, a cough, or a fever. This discovery dovetails with another fast-growing trend we spotted: along with the reality of self-diagnoses comes a major concern for moms that they not overdose their children. These moms were very opposed to treating their kids with medicines that attack the symptoms the kids did not exhibit along with the ones that they did.

The convergence of Triaminic's symptom-specific products and the newfound emotional concerns about overdosing provided our *uncommon offering*.

WHAT: *Triaminic provides a wide variety of cold products that are symptom-specific so you can give your child only the medicine he or she needs*

For moms, this means that they no longer have to "overdose" their kids. For Triaminic, this means that moms don't want just one Triaminic product but instead want several different ones in their medicine chests. Triaminic's *uncommon offering* delivers more products on the stores' shelves and a lot more sales for Triaminic.

Now, please look at the **WHO** and **WHAT** statements for Triaminic together, as this is the best way to assure that the brand's *uncommon offering* can be sold to its *core customer*:

WHO: *A mom concerned about the dangers of overdosing her young children who have colds*

WHAT: *Triaminic provides a wide variety of cold products that are symptom-specific so you can give your child only the medicine he or she needs*

You can readily see the tight fit between the first two components in the Growth Discovery Process for Triaminic. This integration between **WHAT** and **WHO** clearly illustrates the way your *uncommon offering* must be linked to your *core customer* in your growth strategy.

All You Need Is LUV

Tangible and emotional benefits can be found and nurtured in any kind of business, even one as seemingly common, cold, and hard-nosed as an airline.

Much has been written by and about the people who lived through the exhilarating pre- and postlaunch periods of Southwest Airlines. Many authors have offered observations and perspectives from afar. But the story has never been told by the CEO of the agency (the Bloom Agency) that not only launched Southwest in the early 1970s but helped it grow during the first 10 thrilling but tense years of its life.

When our agency was hired to launch Southwest, Rollin King, the founder of the airline, met with our strategic, creative, and management teams, and he urged us not to do anything the way other airlines did it. We took his advice.

In the early stages of our planning, all Southwest meetings took place in our offices, as the airline had none and almost no staff members either. Rollin and his longtime legal counsel, Herb Kelleher, were deeply involved in legal and lobbying issues at the time, but they participated at key decision points. The guy running the day-to-day show for Southwest was the rough and tough Lamar Muse, an experienced airline professional who was determined to make Southwest succeed, whatever the cost or risk. Muse, who came out of retirement from his much-loved Texas ranch in order to launch the airline, was smart, action oriented, and more than ready to take chances.

Kevin and Jackie Freiberg, the authors of *Nuts!*, the definitive book on Southwest, described our approach to strategy development very accurately: "With the help of the Bloom Agency, Southwest's original advertising firm, the company set out to define the airline as a woman—a witty, pert, with-it, startling woman." At that time in our agency's life, we found this "personification technique" quite useful in strategy development. In this instance it delivered the now-famous, valuable, and much-honored Southwest theme, "Now there's somebody else up there who loves you."

Let me explain why our strategy was so appropriate to our *core customer.* Southwest's **WHO** was the beleaguered Texas business traveler—almost all men back in those days. Many of these guys were driving long distances to sell their goods and services around Texas because it was the cheapest way to travel. Those who were able to travel the expensive way were paying outrageous sums to fly Braniff Airlines, the dominant carrier in and to Texas that was notoriously unreliable. To make matters worse, Braniff lavished attention on its first-class customers and ignored its back-of-the-plane passengers.

Suddenly for the unbelievably low price of $15 to fly from Dallas to San Antonio, many potential customers could fly for less cost than they could drive. But, exceptional as the offer was, it wasn't just the price that brought them in droves to Southwest's departure gates.

In addition to the low fare, Southwest offered the much-abused Texas male traveler something else—love. Yes, Southwest made sure that this former back-of-the-plane passenger found the caring attention and service he yearned for. In Southwest's airliner cabins, he was cared for by beautiful, sassy, leggy flight attendants (yes, they were all female back then) wearing tight-fitting hot pants and go-go boots. It all sounds dreadfully sexist these days, and perhaps it was, but the times and values were very different back then. In addition to the personal attention, Southwest gave these travelers a powerful tangible benefit they could always count on: on-time performance.

In sum, Texas's drivers and flyers alike wanted someone to care about them and pay attention to their travel needs—yes, someone to love them. "Love" was the *uncommon offering*—offered over and over again—in TV, on radio, on billboards, and in every touch point with Southwest's customers.

Love and low-cost on-time performance—perhaps the world's most perfect emotional and tangible benefits. If you have any doubts about whether Southwest is still embracing and benefiting from our strategy, check out its New York Stock Exchange ticker symbol—LUV.

Keep It Fresh and New

What Triaminic and Southwest did and what you will need to do is deliver your *uncommon offering* (remember—not common and not unique) consistently and with lots of imagination, always keeping it fresh and relevant so current customers will remain loyal to the company and new customers will be attracted to try its products or services. The business idea that you embraced when you launched your company or the one that informs your department, division, or brand must continue to be enhanced as you reach each stage of your growth cycle. The business's *uncommon offering*—its **WHAT**—must never become obsolete.

Some companies and brands become obsolete almost overnight and some over many years. Let's take a quick look at two iconic global brands that have not consistently invigorated their *uncommon offering*, that have paid the penalty in terms of tumbling revenues and lost market share, and that are now attempting to remedy their situations.

Ford Taurus was once the bestselling car in America. In 1986, when it was introduced to the U.S. domestic market, as related by the *Wall Street Journal*, its fresh, contemporary look, front-wheel drive, and aerodynamic design gave it a striking appearance and feel in contrast to the boxy look of most American cars at the time. Consumers rewarded Ford for its innovation—its *uncommon offering*. But as years passed, Ford failed to refresh and renew its offering. In the words of Ford's current CEO, Alan Mulally, the Taurus "was dynamite and an industry leader. But then we stopped investing in it." The Taurus fell into irrelevance and diminishing sales, and it was finally retired from the market in 2006. An automotive writer recently described the Taurus as "the car credited for reinvigorating American automotive design two decades ago before falling into virtual irrelevance by the time it was retired last year. . . . In its final years, the Taurus was merely an also-ran." Ford is attempting to reintroduce the Taurus for the 2008 model year. Can the company breathe new life into an old, faded offering? No one knows the answer, but the company certainly has its work cut out for it.

> **The business idea that you embraced when you launched your company or the one that informs your department, division, or brand must continue to be enhanced as you reach each stage of your growth cycle.**

Eastman Kodak, maker of one of the most well known products in the world—the small yellow box of film—has suffered long and publicly in the face of the digital revolution's onslaught. With layoffs and restructuring, the once-great photographic materials and equipment company is shrinking itself in an effort to become profitable once again. As the *Wall Street Journal* sees it, the company's declining fortunes reflect "the continued shrinkage of Kodak's former cash cow—its film and photo-processing operations—as consumers shift to digital photography."

To fully understand the common problem these once great companies and brands face, please reexamine the explanations offered by journalists covering the stories: "In its final years, the Taurus was merely an also-ran." "Continued shrinkage of Kodak's former cash cow—its film and photo-processing operations—as consumers shift to digital photography."

Why weren't the early signs of "irrelevance" noticed by managements of these enormous companies long before they became realities? How can you prevent such a disastrous situation in your company?

Here's how. At the very first sign—or even before the first sign—that sales of your product, service, company, or brand are slowing down, start thinking about irrelevance. Immediately examine your *uncommon offering* and begin to develop ways to revitalize it. After all, your *uncommon offering* is your very reason for being. Irrelevance is the path to obsolescence, and resurrecting a brand or company is perhaps the *most* difficult task in the business world.

Savvy marketers consistently refresh their *uncommon offering*. BMW reconfigures the designs of its cars and brings out new models on a regular schedule. L'Oréal routinely launches new and improved products with different ingredients, aromas, colors, and packaging. T.G.I. Friday's constantly introduces fun-sounding new dishes. Starbucks features new beverages and snacks every season— for example, pumpkin in the fall and berry coolers in the summer. FedEx introduced an entirely new service model, FedEx Ground, and added new services near many of its customers with its acquisition of Kinko's, now called FedEx Kinko's.

I urge you to follow these winning examples of renewal to assure that your *uncommon offering*—your **WHAT**—never becomes obsolete.

Create an Unbreakable Bond with Your Customers

It is important to understand your business's customer touch points in relation to your *uncommon offering*. Your customers and potential customers come in contact with your products or services many times; a few of these are "make or break" moments in your emotional relationship with them.

Give serious thought to the key touch points in your business. One touch point is initial exposure to your firm. Let customers see and feel the essence of your *uncommon offering* when they first walk through your door or phone for information about a product or service or visit your Web site. The same is true of other initial exposures to your firm such as your store window, Web site, or Yellow Pages listing or advertising. Another touch point is the moment when the customer is seriously considering a purchase from you—this is the most critical moment to connect with that person emotionally, perhaps in the context of the all-important price of your product or the valuable service you offer after the sale.

Still other touch points where you can connect emotionally with a customer occur when your product or service is being used. This is the moment to reinforce the essence of your company's *uncommon offering* with a follow up e-mail, personal letter, or phone call. Another way to demonstrate that your customers' opinions are valuable is a customer satisfaction questionnaire. Later in the book, I'll show you how to infuse all these touch points with positive experiences that will become an important part of your Inside Advantage.

Now, though, it's time to turn to the task of identifying the *uncommon offering* in your own business.

CHAPTER 6

Dig Deep for Your Advantage

Now I'd like to help you, as I have helped my clients over the years, discover, define, and articulate the sustainable *uncommon offering* you can use to grow your business.

We'll be creating a **WHAT** statement of approximately 10 carefully chosen, simple, and vivid words that express your company's *uncommon offering*—the most influential component in your Growth Discovery Process. As with your **WHO** statement, each word must be chosen with exceptional care. We'll then make sure that your **WHAT** and your **WHO** statements work together perfectly.

To help you consider ways to define your business's *uncommon offering* we'll go inside another client consulting session, this time with a prominent Texas wealth management services company.

Having been introduced to this firm by an important client, I decided to undertake this assignment, as I thought it sounded like an interesting one. The company's senior management wanted to initiate a mass media advertising campaign to drive its growth in Texas. With my lifetime of experience in the advertising business, I've come to believe that advertising is *not* always the way to spur profitable growth. We shall see.

I found myself very interested in developing this firm's *uncommon offering* because it was operating in a field that harbored what seemed to me to be a lot of undifferentiated offerings. So there was potential as well as an interesting challenge here. In order to find an Inside Advantage, we'd need first to get the offering right. For my rendition of our working session, see "A Bob Bloom Consulting Session—Finding Our **WHAT**," which follows.

A BOB BLOOM CONSULTING SESSION

Finding Our WHAT

The first thing I notice when I walk into the room is that there are over 30 people here—far too many for everyone to actively participate. But we move forward with the rules of the session, the purpose of the charts, and a description of the Growth Discovery Process.

We then begin to generate the many words and phrases that depict the customer of this company. (I'm giving you an overview of this part of the entire process so we can focus on our search for the *uncommon offering*.) I quickly understand that its customer is not your everyday Joe or Jane—it's an exceptionally wealthy person or family. The company will only accept customers with more than $15 million to invest. Wow! I say to myself. I ask all participants to create a picture in their head of their single most important customer (which, as you now know, will be useful in recruiting new customers). After they give a lot of bland descriptive terms, something interesting happens as I push them for more vivid ways to describe this individual. The group starts throwing out these words to portray this current customer: *demanding, spoiled, difficult*, and *lazy*. I now begin to see this very rich, perhaps arrogant person in my head.

After the normal give and take, we begin our customer statement with the requisite definition: *a prospective client* [the company's term for *customer*] *with assets of $15 + million to invest*. The statement is a little long, but each word is essential. (Remember—this is not a word count game, although brevity is also essential.)

We struggle to find words to depict this target customer in an accurate but not disrespectful way, moving away from terms like *spoiled* to ones like *demanding*. Many phrases are generated and we start writing, editing, and abbreviating until we find the right words to complete the **WHO** statement: *and an intense desire for special services and attention*.

We all agree that we have done a very good job of defining our *core customer*.

WHO: *A prospective client with assets of $15+ million to invest plus an intense desire for special services and attention*

We take a midmorning break and reassemble to define **WHAT**. We fill many charts with the various investment services the company provides its clients. The services all seem quite typical for this sort of business. I push the group to identify the more exceptional services it provides its clients. Suddenly, from the back of the room I hear "rich-boys toys!" "What are 'rich-boys toys'?'" I ask the room. Someone comes back at me with "airplanes!" Another yells out "ranches!" Still others pipe up with "oil fields!"

I'm starting to get a picture, but not a complete one, so I have to ask the obvious questions: "What about these 'toys'? What do you do to help your clients with their airplanes, ranches, and oil fields?" The answers are interesting. Several members of the group begin explaining: the firm actually manages these personal properties for its clients, helping them with everything from paying bills to negotiating maintenance contracts to providing advice concerning the sale or trade of the properties. I then ask another pertinent question, "Do any of your competitors provide these services for their customers?" The answer is a resounding "No! They just invest their clients' money."

Bingo! We've found an *uncommon offering* and now have the ammunition we need to write a compelling **WHAT** statement.

We generate words that can describe these special services without merely listing them. I hear terms like *group of services* and *suite of services* before we start moving in a better direction with good words we all like such as *unrivaled portfolio of customized services*. We move on to define the firm's conventional investing services and the right words, *exceptional investment results*, come quite easily, but there is a long debate regarding the sequence of the phrases in the statement. Some people want to put the *customized services* part before *exceptional investment results*. Others want to go the other way. I step in and convince them to lead with the services that will differentiate them from the competition. We all agree that the following *uncommon offering*, while long, has clarity and freshness: *an expert financial advisor who delivers an unrivaled portfolio of customized services and exceptional investment results*. The words *customized* and *results* added the emotional content the statement needs. As we did with Triaminic (and every time the Growth Discovery Process is used), we test the integration of **WHAT** with **WHO**, and we all feel that they fit together perfectly.

WHO: *A prospective client with assets of $15+ million to invest plus an intense desire for special services and attention*

WHAT: *An expert financial advisor who delivers an unrivaled portfolio of customized services and exceptional investment results*

This client's initial interest in mass media to reach a virtual handful of rich Texans who need customized services would have been both unproductive and wasteful. Later in the book, I'll show you better and more effective strategies for reaching out to the most appropriate customer and persuading him or her to buy from your business.

Finding Your WHAT

Now that you understand the importance of **WHAT**, you're probably eager to discover your own business's *uncommon offering*. As I did in your search for your *core customer*, I'll provide you with a step-by-step procedure that will enable you to define the *uncommon offering* you can own and leverage. I urge you to give each and every step some serious time and consideration. Each is designed to encourage objective thinking, assure that you look far beyond the narrow transaction between you and your customer, create an offering that will both *help* and *inspire* your customers, and deliver a meaningful, beneficial experience at every customer touch point.

1. Begin with a thorough review of the **WHO** you described in Part 1 of the book, because, as I've said before, your **WHAT** must be sold to your **WHO**.

2. Next—and this is really important—do *not* start drafting the description of your *uncommon offering* right away. Rather, make a list of *all* the potential offerings that now exist inside your business, not just your favorites—and certainly not those you wish you had or want to have in the future. Your list must be realistic as well as comprehensive. Seek some objective thoughts and observations from people who know your business. Ask employees, vendors, advisors, and customers—especially your most important customer—to tell you, very candidly, what makes your company different and perhaps better than your competitors.

3. Carefully examine your complete list of offerings, especially those that provide the emotional assurance your customers seek. Circle those few that offer the potential to retain your current customers and, importantly, attract new customers in sufficient quantity to drive your profitable growth. It's premature to land on any single offering.

4. Ask yourself these six questions about *each* offering on your short list:

   • Is it already owned, in part or whole, by a competitor? Eliminate any option that is not uncommon.

   • Is it discrete—really different from the others on your list, or is it saying the same thing in another way? Eliminate all duplications.

   • Could it be combined with another option on your list to make a single more powerful offering? But don't make the mistake of creating a combination offering that is longer, more complex, and less clear. Eliminate those potential offerings that are not compelling enough to stand alone.

   • Will it be enduring, or is its appeal based on an idea that has a short shelf life? Eliminate any offering that can't stand the test of time.

   • Of the remaining options, which *single* offering will enable you to deliver a meaningful, beneficial experience at every customer touch point? Eliminate those that fail this test.

   • Of the options that remain, is there one that delivers the emotional assurance your most important customer needs to remain loyal to your firm? If so, this is very likely your *uncommon offering* and ultimately your Inside Advantage!

5. Now it's time to begin drafting a statement that expresses your *uncommon offering*. Don't be concerned with the length of the statement right now. You're looking for words or phrases

that describe your offering in a clear, simple, and fresh way. Avoid words that are fancy or industry jargon or that sound like a slogan. This is not a "vision" or a "mission" statement or advertising copy—this is a realistic **WHAT** that you must sell to your customers to grow your business. Your statement must define the tangible benefits as well as the emotional customer experience you can deliver today and tomorrow. It must be real and not merely wishful thinking. You don't want to create *an image of difference*—you want to *be honestly and truly different*. Keep working on this statement until it is brief, accurate, and precise. Anyone who reads it should understand it right away.

6. Take a few minutes to ensure that your **WHO** statement links tightly with your new **WHAT** statement because your *core customer* must want to buy your *uncommon offering*.

> You don't want to create *an image of difference*–you want to *be honestly and truly different*.

7. Before proceeding, take a close look at the **WHO** and **WHAT** statements that follow. They were created in sessions with my consulting clients. Observe them only as a model and only for inspiration. Please don't copy them, because each is specific to its business. Compare your statement with any of the ones shown, *not* in content but in the way it communicates its individual *uncommon offering*. I've provided statements from the same companies you saw in an earlier chapter: companies of various sizes and types, including B2B, high-tech, retail, not-for-profit, and consumer products and services. Your business is different from every other business—including the ones discussed in this book—and it will only grow if your *uncommon offering* is absolutely true to your firm's own customer experience.

Core Customer WHO and WHAT Statements

A National Chain of Suburban Newspapers

WHO: An active suburban homeowning family that cares about enhancing its quality of life and learning about local products and services that satisfy its needs and wants

WHAT: Timely, valuable news and information that touches the lives of the local community more consistently and comprehensively than any other source

A West Coast Golf Products Retailer

WHO: An affluent, avid golfer who constantly seeks a better golfing experience

WHAT: Expert advice, customized assistance, and a passion for helping our clients improve their game

A Global Technology Provider

WHO: A global business enterprise that seeks the expert advice of a technology provider that understands its business

WHAT: A trusting partnership that ensures operational efficiency and valuable intelligence from its customers' technology investment

A Renowned Symphony Orchestra

WHO: A frequent patron of classical music concerts who seeks a more passionate musical experience

WHAT: An orchestra that encourages every musician to share in the creation of an intensely memorable concert

An Ultra-High-End Jewelry Store

WHO: An affluent local male or female status seeker who is looking for a fashion statement

not a word count drill. Keep working in your session to eliminate unnecessary words, avoid word duplication, and seek clarity. Move the words around to see if the statement is shorter or clearer. Get some perspective from your associates or someone you respect. Above all, in as few words as possible, create a business offering that is uncommon and that will drive profitable growth.

Q: Is the **WHAT** statement really just a tagline or a slogan?

A: Absolutely not. It is the way to convert your *uncommon offering* into user-friendly language; that user is you and those in your business unit. The customer will never see these words—however, he or she may see an expression of your *uncommon offering* in the form of a tagline or slogan. The language of your **WHAT** statement is an internal commitment you and your firm are making to your external customer audience—it is not an external expression. This is not a mission statement or a vision statement and it is certainly not a tagline or slogan. Remember what I said earlier in this chapter: you're not trying to create a mere image of difference—you want to be truly different. Taglines and slogans are good devices some of the time but not always. A great tagline might help you succeed if, for example, you own a store similar to our ultra-high-end jewelry store, but it won't prevent your failure. Sometimes a tagline is inconsistent with a category or industry, as it would be with a symphony orchestra or a law firm. Nike, Apple, and Tiffany don't have slogans because they are recognized by their famous symbols—the swoosh, an apple, and little blue box. Here's why—they have powerful *uncommon offerings* that they deliver on day in and day out. Yes, *uncommon offerings* can be translated into meaningful, relevant slogans, but it is the essence of the *uncommon offering* itself that you want your target customer to remember and believe.

Q: I understand the need to "help" my customers, but I'm not sure I really get the idea of "inspiring" them. What does *inspire* really mean?

A: When you deliver your *uncommon offering* to your customer, you *help* that customer. He or she will *benefit* in some way from your product or service. At the same moment, that customer will have some kind of emotional experience—positive or negative—from the interaction with the business or its product or service. Perhaps it's just a small positive experience when you say "thank you" or a big positive one when you tell the customer that you will complete the construction of a new building well in advance of when it was promised. On the other hand, a customer attempting to check into a hotel certainly will have an unexpected negative experience when told that, in spite of his confirmed reservation, the hotel is overbooked and can't accommodate him. If you happen to be in the lodging business, you should have policies in place to have the customer driven to a good hotel nearby and given a certificate for a complimentary room in your hotel on his next visit to your city. It may be possible to *inspire* those customers with your care and concern for them even under very difficult circumstances. The idea is to *inspire* your customers to have a positive experience at every touch point in their relationship with your firm. Anticipate their needs and preferences—*inspire* them to have a positive emotional experience with your company each and every time.

With everything you've learned about **WHO** and **WHAT**, you're more than halfway toward unleashing your Inside Advantage.

BLOOM ON GROWTH

> The idea is to *inspire* your customers to have a positive experience at every touch point in their relationship with your firm.

Now that you know how to create an *uncommon offering*, you may be wondering how you're going to sell this **WHAT** to your customer—your **WHO**. You'll make this sale just like you make any sale—you'll be persuasive. Let's now turn to Part 3, where you'll discover **HOW** to persuade **WHO** to purchase **WHAT**.

Persuasive Strategies

HOW Do You Convince Them?

HOW

CHAPTER 7

A Platform Built for One

Imagine a giant table on which you and all your competitors can stand. You are surrounded by potential customers, and each of your rivals is shouting his or her *uncommon offering*. The result is a lot of noise and total customer confusion.

Now imagine that instead of joining this group of adversaries on the big table, you are standing nearby on a small, but extraordinarily sturdy table that can hold only you. You stand out. You seem different because you are different—different from your competitors. Customers notice you and hear you. This small, sturdy table is the *persuasive strategy* that will enable you to convince your *core customer* to buy your *uncommon offering* instead of all other competitors' offerings. The success of your business depends on your acknowledgment and true understanding of the fact that all businesses, big and small, compete with other businesses for customers.

On the surface, this statement doesn't appear very surprising or profound, yet most managers and owners seem to forget it, or don't understand it, or don't plan their growth strategies with it in mind. The penalty for not running a business with this reality firmly in mind can be severe and can include a loss of opportunities, customers, and even the failure of their businesses.

You are constantly surrounded by ambitious competitors. Every hungry competitor is, in fact, chasing the very same potential customer you are. Don't make the mistake that many businesspeople do in thinking that all you have to do is "build a better mousetrap" and customers will beat a path to your door. With apologies to Ralph Waldo Emerson, don't fall for the notion that potential customers are going to find their way to you unaided and unguided. Your business won't grow if you don't make it your primary job to *persuade* customers that your mousetrap—your *uncommon offering*—provides them with tangible and emotional benefits ideally suited to their needs and desires.

That imperative applies no matter how terrific your *uncommon offering* is: you must have a *persuasive strategy* to convince your *core customer* to buy your *uncommon offering* instead of all other competitors' offerings. In terms of my Growth Discovery Process, this way of standing out, this approach to differentiation, is your **HOW**. Once you have the right *persuasive strategy* in place, you have taken the vitally important step of differentiating your business from all competitors' businesses.

> Don't make the mistake that many businesspeople do in thinking that all you have to do is "build a better mousetrap" and customers will beat a path to your door.

Your Persuasive Strategy—HOW

Let's turn again to the equation for the Growth Discovery Process and take a look at the way **HOW** interacts with **WHO, WHAT,** and **OWN IT!** Having established your *core customer* and your *uncommon offering*, you turn to your *persuasive strategy*, the means by which you differentiate your business from the competitors' businesses.

WHO + WHAT + HOW + OWN IT! = INSIDE ADVANTAGE

WHO is the *core customer* most likely to buy your product or service in the quantity required for optimal profit.

WHAT is the *uncommon offering* that your business will own and leverage.

HOW is the *persuasive strategy* that will convince your *core customer* to buy your *uncommon offering* versus all competitive offerings.

OWN IT! is the series of *imaginative acts* that will celebrate your *uncommon offering* and make it well known to your *core customer*.

In the chapters that follow, I'll show you how to construct a highly influential and effective **HOW**. I'll show you how to make it true, honest, and strong and to reflect the realities of your business. Your *persuasive strategy* cannot be made up or fake—if it is, it might work for a short while, until you are found out, at which point you will lose your customers, your reputation, and any hope of growing your business.

It must also be credible and easily understood by both current and potential customers. This *persuasive strategy* must also be tightly integrated with the other components of your Growth Discovery Process because **HOW** will enable you to sell **WHAT** to **WHO**. Your growth ambition can only be realized with a brief, simple, and believable **HOW**.

Let's now take a look at some real-life examples of **HOW**— *persuasive strategies* at work in the marketplace.

 BLOOM ON GROWTH Your *persuasive strategy* cannot be made up or fake— if it is, it might work for a short while, until you are found out, at which point you will lose your customers, your reputation, and any hope of growing your business.

Persuasive Strategies for Hard-to-Please Customers

When our agency was hired by the big Swiss drug company Sandoz (now a part of Novartis) we were asked to evaluate a cold medicine, successful in Switzerland and Canada, but not showing much promise in its U.S. test market. This product, branded NeoCitran, was made up of very strong, cold- and flu-fighting ingredients. Unlike traditional capsules, pills, and liquids, NeoCitran was a citrus-flavored powder in a packet that, when dissolved in hot water, tea, or broth treated many severe symptoms such as fever, cough, chills, headache, muscle ache, and fatigue.

The Swiss and Canadian customers enjoyed the taste of their citrus-flavored hot liquids and found hot beverages soothing and warming in their cold climates. Moreover, they found the medicine's ingredients powerful and therapeutic. However in the United States, NeoCitran's powder in a packet and citrus flavor was a nonstarter, despite its powerful inherent promise: *a strong and comforting cold medicine formulated with ingredients to treat many severe flulike symptoms such as fever, cough, chills, headache, muscle ache, and fatigue.*

In the context of my Growth Discovery Process, this excellent product had a compelling *uncommon offering*, a start, at least on our way to developing its Inside Advantage. But how could we overcome U.S. customers' negative attitudes toward hot, citrus-flavored beverages and the product's unfamiliar brand name? And how could we persuade customers to go to all the trouble of opening a packet, boiling some water, and mixing the drink when they could simply pop a pill or down some liquid medicine? We all recognized that the next step toward the brand's Inside Advantage required a brilliant strategy—one so persuasive that Americans would recognize the healing benefits of NeoCitran's great strengths and effectiveness and buy it regardless of its form, taste, and inconvenience!

To solve this almost overwhelming challenge we looked more closely at our *core customer*—we wanted to better understand what made the American cold or flu sufferer different from the Canadian and Swiss customer. We knew that Americans weren't accustomed to sipping a lot of hot "comfort" drinks. But another American cultural tendency seemed potentially relevant: Americans prefer the biggest and most powerful form of almost everything. Our DNA screams, "We're a big country with big people, so bring on those mammoth cars, giant corporations, powerful athletes, and enormous burgers." We are the extra-big, extra-powerful, extra-strength society.

We had a hunch that Americans would go for an extra-strength medicine that treated the very worst symptoms of colds and flu. We believed that Americans' preference for heavy-duty, extra-strength everything would overcome the barriers to purchasing NeoCitran if and only if we could create an "extra-strength" *persuasive strategy* with this American customer in mind. In the terms of the Growth Discovery Process, we needed a powerful **HOW** that would accurately reflect the best of the product: the *uncommon offering* we had discovered.

We crafted a *persuasive strategy* that went like this: *convince an ailing cold sufferer to try a new extra-strength, highly therapeutic medicine that provides soothing, healing relief from severe flulike symptoms.* Our client agreed with this strategy, and the consumers we talked to confirmed that we were on target. Confident of our compelling strategy, we moved forward with the development of our ad campaign.

As we were working, a member of our team said, "too bad that the brand name doesn't have 'flu' in it." That seemingly naïve idea got our attention, but we felt that it would never fly with the client. As it turned out, we had underestimated our client's determination to grow its brand by achieving success in the huge U.S. market. Our client declared itself open to the idea *if* we could come up with a new name that would be approved by government authorities and if we could provide evidence that it was persuasive enough to motivate customers to try it. We tested some ways to add *flu* to the NeoCitran brand name, such as putting *flu* in front or back of it, and we created some entirely new names. The overwhelming winner of the brand renaming for the United States was Theraflu, a joining of *therapy* and *flu* in a way that suggested that the medicine would provide relief for the flu sufferer. Following the approval of the new brand name, test markets provided the incontrovertible evidence we were seeking—Theraflu was a winner.

Thanks to our client's determination to grow its business, Theraflu became a big success. Today, it is still powered by this same *persuasive strategy*, and cold sufferers can find Theraflu in almost every store in the United States that sells drug products.

Creating the right **HOW** statement for your product or service can give you similar results—and you probably don't have to change anything about the business. But like our client, you do have to be determined to grow your business with a strong *persuasive strategy*.

T.G.I. Friday's was determined to grow its business by using a *persuasive strategy* that looked like this: *own the idea that every day in the week is a "Thank God It's Friday" day and can be celebrated at and only at Friday's*.

And BMW was determined to grow its business by using a *persuasive strategy* that was equally strong: *create vehicles that are highly valued because they are uncompromising, authentic, and exhilarating to drive*.

Combat Commoditization with Persuasive Strategies

I don't believe that any service or product is a "commodity." Of course, commoditization can and does occur, but only when a firm *allows it to happen*. SKF, a Swedish company that the *Financial Times* calls the world's largest maker of industrial bearings, is one firm that has fought successfully against commoditization.

Bearings are the little metal balls or cylinders that minimize the effects of friction and keep parts of machines moving smoothly. They are simple items, easy to manufacture, and easy to copy. As the *Financial Times* points out, "the bearings business is highly susceptible to the threat of commoditization, in which manufacturers in low-cost economies take market share by selling cheap copies of basic products."

How can a company in such an industry beat the low-cost producers? In the case of SKF, its CEO, Tom Johnstone, set out to make the technology and the expertise hidden deep inside the company available to his customers. The company's sales engineers began bringing customers and the experts together to work as a team to "discover customers' requirements and line them up with the right technical solution, often customized for their needs." Johnstone's term for the process is "knowledge engineering . . . technical know-how applied in a targeted way."

BLOOM ON GROWTH

> I don't believe that any service or product is a "commodity." Of course, commoditization can and does occur, but only when a firm *allows it to happen.*

What a great way to articulate this idea that, in Johnstone's words, can "solve the problems of our customers, add value to our product, and also shield ourselves from competitors." This is a fresh way to explain that a company's strategy must benefit both the company and its customers.

With our similar approaches to growth, I feel that Mr. Johnstone and I would get along well in business. Were I asked to articulate SKF's *persuasive strategy*, I would suggest the following: *solve the special needs of each customer by directly and consistently involving our sales, development, and production teams with their management and technical experts.*

However Mr. Johnstone might phrase his *persuasive strategy*, it seems to be getting the job done, as the *Financial Times* reports that "in 2005, pre-tax profits rose 29% in 2005 and were up another 12% in the first nine months of 2006." Do these numbers look like SKF is victim of commoditization?

When any company, including "commodity" companies like SKF, can deliver its customers a service they want and need, two important benefits make themselves felt: First, offering a highly valued service insulates a company from having to compete exclusively on price. Second, the service enhances the potential for an enduring customer relationship because the customer wants to continue to receive the service and may come to rely on it. This lesson should be of particular interest to you if you are in a business squeezed by cut-rate competition or experiencing a high customer turnover.

Persuasive Strategies That Beat the Heat

In an earlier chapter you met Stanley Marcus, the business genius behind the Neiman Marcus retailing empire. At one point while building his business, he came to realize he was facing a severe problem, a real challenge to his store's growth: his sales suffered terribly during the exceptionally hot Texas summers. Unlike fashion emporiums in milder climates, Neiman Marcus's sales slump began in the summer and continued into the warm months of

September and October. Customers would simply wait for November and December to shop for and purchase expensive gowns, furs, jewelry, and fancy men's wear. Continuing to suffer through such a difficult seasonal pattern would keep Nieman Marcus from generating profitable growth.

BLOOM ON GROWTH

Offering a highly valued service insulates a company from having to compete exclusively on price. The service enhances the potential for an enduring customer relationship because the customer wants to continue to receive the service and may come to rely on it.

Stanley Marcus could simply have allowed the unfavorable seasonal Texas climate to destroy his growth ambition or he could have initiated remedial action. He did the latter: he decided to create what the retail industry aptly calls an "artificial" event, one created by the store, not by the calendar. He invented a ground-breaking promotional event—one that has often been copied but to this day remains unrivaled in the world of retailing. Its primary purpose was to create numerous festive social occasions in Dallas during the slow selling season to stimulate the purchase of expensive apparel, jewelry, and furs.

The promotional events he created were named "Fortnights" to add to his invented events the panache of the British expression for a 14-day period. These unprecedented Fortnights are superb examples of the kinds of *imaginative acts* I'll be discussing in Part 4. In that part you will find all of the lavish details of these events that were created with pure commercial intent but implemented with the distinctive style and sophistication of Stanley Marcus. Here, however, we want to focus on the *persuasive strategy* behind these remarkable events.

Let's see what we can learn about developing an effective **HOW** statement for your business by studying what Stanley might have envisioned as his *persuasive strategy* for the innovative Neiman Marcus promotional idea:

HOW: *Celebrate the tradition, culture, craftsmanship, and fashion of a famous nation in a 14-day October event that will captivate our clientele, create festive occasions for chic attire, and generate acclaim for our brand*

I want to be clear that these are my words, not Stanley's. While a little long, the statement is both specific and vivid. It is limited to *how* the strategy will be achieved, not *what* tactics will be employed to implement the strategy. Tactics are the imaginative territory of **OWN IT!**, and the subject of Part 4.

But Stanley Marcus didn't stop there. He also did what no one else had ever done or probably will ever do—he created an entirely new promotional "medium." To attract and keep customers coming to his store, enhance his holiday sales, and create a worldwide buzz, he published a highly fashionable Christmas catalog that featured a secret, unprecedented gift idea to be unveiled in the catalog, such as his-and-her submarines, his-and-her airplanes, his-and-her traditional Chinese boats called junks, and other equally outrageous superexpensive gifts. Once again, to illustrate how a *persuasive strategy* can work in the marketplace, I've created a **HOW** statement that Stanley might have envisioned:

HOW: *Originate a Christmas gift so magical, expensive, and unexpected that it will compel anticipation for and readership of our Christmas catalog and inspire annual international press coverage for our brand at the Christmas season*

Through *persuasive strategies* focused on his *core customer*— well-to-do, fashion-conscious men and women living in or visiting the Dallas area, eager to display the symbols of their success to the world—Stanley Marcus built a vast retail business and a distinctive international reputation for imagination, sophistication, and fashion.

Persuasive Strategy for Transforming a Brand

There's a lot of magic in the sort of retailing espoused by Stanley Marcus, and if you have the imagination and the money, the sky is the limit. But what about less-glamorous businesses? What about companies with more mundane products and services such as those that offer technology or communication services? Companies in down-to-earth industries can also create effective strategies for building and growing their businesses or brands. Here's how one company that I worked with very closely used a *persuasive strategy* specifically constructed to confront a severe challenge and transform it into an opportunity.

T-Mobile, the cellular telephone and wireless Internet services company, at one time needed to change its well-established U.S. brand name (VoiceStream) to adopt its parent company's global brand name (T-Mobile). There is no more vulnerable time for a company than when it's changing its brand name.

During a brand name change, a company is in danger of losing its current customers, because no one likes change, and new customers are reluctant to switch to an unfamiliar brand. Most companies opt for a transition period—they phase out the old brand and phase in the new brand with advertising that tries to justify the name change and persuade customers and potential customers that they will benefit from the move. All too often this expensive "phased" strategy simply prolongs the period of vulnerability and increases the company's risk.

BLOOM ON GROWTH

> There is no more vulnerable time for a company than when it's changing its brand name.

Robert Dotson, T-Mobile's aggressive CEO, had the marketing savvy and courage to choose a different path. All across America, area by area, the system changeover and store makeover were instantaneous. The company's advertising utilized the famous face and familiar personality of Catherine Zeta-Jones. T-Mobile's TV, print ads, and point of sale described the brand's global reach, customer benefits, and special offers as if the T-Mobile brand had been around forever—just as if, like its spokesperson, it was already famous and familiar. T-Mobile customers were notified just before the start of advertising, but there was no mention of the brand name change in the ads for the company. T-Mobile secured its huge customer base and attracted new customers in record numbers because its **HOW** was persuasive as well as assumptive—and brave.

Had Robert Dotson committed to paper the *persuasive strategy* he was perusing throughout the transition phase, I've no doubt it would read like this:

> **HOW:** *Confidently promote T-Mobile's global reach, valuable benefits, and compelling offers as if the brand were already famous and familiar by using a famous and familiar spokesperson*

Whether you're selling a so-called commodity product—traditional restaurant foods and beverages, one of many automobile brands, a conventional technology service, a typical cold product, or retail merchandise—you can grow your company by crafting a *persuasive strategy* that will leverage your Inside Advantage. Just remember that the single-minded purpose of **HOW** is to create the strategy that will differentiate you from the competitors and convince customers to buy your product or service instead of the competitors'.

Speaking of competitive offers, let's turn our focus to the nature of competition in business and how to use *persuasive strategies* to gain the upper hand over even your toughest competitors.

CHAPTER 8

Stand Out by Standing Alone

W e've all observed people walking down the street with thin white wires coming out of their ears—their heads are bobbing, their shoulders are swaying, and they're singing out loud. They are animated beings. And they are animated because they are listening to their iPods.

It's testimony to the way iPod stands alone in the world on its own small, sturdy "table" at this moment in time, with a powerful offering and an innovative strategic platform. Apple has successfully demonstrated that millions of people can be transformed by a very personal connection to music because it "animates" their lives. By standing alone and away from the competition, iPod and the business it has generated has almost doubled the size of Apple, in an astonishingly short period of time.

The *Wall Street Journal* has flatteringly described Apple's products, and the phenomena they generate, as "the Apple II, the world's first personal computer, as we would come to understand the term; the Macintosh, the world's most influential computer; and now, of course, the iPod, the technical/fashion accessory/lifestyle hybrid that belongs in any time capsule trying to explain what life in the early 21st century was like."

Year after year and with product after product, Apple has accomplished the feat of never directly competing with rivals on size or function. I'll describe the special way they do this—how they OWN IT!—in Part 4. But for now, I'd like to point out the enormous benefits of standing alone.

The biggest dividend of standing alone and avoiding the competition is that competitors have to travel a treacherous road—not to surpass you but merely to catch up. Look at the way Microsoft is struggling to catch up with the success of Apple. At the end of its 2007 second quarter, Apple reported an 88 percent increase in profits from the same period a year ago. Sales during the period were just as stunning: 10.5 million iPods (a total of 100 million to date) and 1.5 million Macs. According to CEO Steve Jobs, this was "more than three times the industry growth rate." Commenting on this extraordinary performance, Eugene A. Munster, an analyst at Piper Jaffray, said, "They're defying the laws of gravity."

Another big dividend of standing alone is the clout it gives you with potential strategic partners. Apple has been able to make good deals with the music companies and is currently pushing for better ones. And it has been lining up Hollywood studios in new partnerships that allow Apple to sell films through the iTunes store. Partnerships with Paramount Pictures, MGM, and other film companies have made hundreds of films available for download by iPod users.

Yet another benefit of standing alone and avoiding competition is the wake it leaves for new-product entries by the same company. The introduction of Apple's new mobile telephone, the iPhone, was widely and impatiently anticipated. As the *Financial Times* puts it, the unveiling of the iPhone "was greeted by rapturous applause, gasps of disbelief and occasional whoops of joy from the Apple faithful."

While standing alone offers many benefits, companies like Apple, whose future relies on a constant stream of new, unique offerings, face a rocky road with very high tolls. As we discussed in an earlier chapter, it's a challenging, costly, and risky addiction that, more often than not, ends in disaster. There are exceptions, of course, and Apple is clearly one of them. However let's don't lose sight of one pretty obvious reality: Apple is led by Steve Jobs, one of the most brilliant innovators and marketers on the planet. So, mere mortals like myself—and perhaps you—should stick to achieving growth in a more practical and sure way. And that, of course, is what the Growth Discovery Process is designed to do.

A good, effective *persuasive strategy*—your **HOW**—does not promise you that you can *avoid* competition the way Steve Jobs does, but it does promote a way to succeed versus *all the competitive offerings*. As a writer in *The Economist* put it, "If you are the first to discover a tree, you get to pick the lowest-hanging fruit." Think of **HOW** as a way that will help you get to the tree first.

What Makes a Persuasive Strategy Persuasive?

There are five hallmarks of a good *persuasive strategy*:

1. It must be action-oriented, not just a vague promise or sincere commitment.

2. It must define the specific action right up front; the first word must always be an active verb.

3. It must be strategic, not tactical—it must state "what" your product will actually do, not "how" the product will do it.

4. It must be honest and achievable, not imagined and unaffordable.

5. It must be tightly integrated with your definition of the *core customer* and the reality of your *uncommon offering*.

Let's return to our Triaminic and Juicy Juice examples and examine the ways their **HOW** might be defined in the context of each of these five hallmarks of a good *persuasive strategy*.

Triaminic

WHO: *A mom concerned about the dangers of overdosing her young children who have colds*

WHAT: *Triaminic provides a wide variety of cold products that are symptom-specific so you can give your child only the medicine he or she needs*

HOW: *Help Mom select the symptom-specific Triaminic formula that has only the medicine her child needs to get well as quickly as possible*

Now let's drill down into the Triaminic **HOW** statement and take a closer look at the words and phrases we are using:

1. "Help Mom" is action-oriented.

2. "Help" also defines a specific action because it speaks directly to Mom's need for assistance.

3. Helping her "select the symptom-specific Triaminic formula" strategically states what the product will actually do in its communications to the target customer.

4. Providing formulas that have "only the medicine her child needs to get well as quickly as possible" is an honest and achievable promise. The product is designed to deliver on this promise.

5. As you can see, this *persuasive strategy* couldn't be any more tightly linked with the *core customer* "Mom" and the *uncommon offering* "symptom-specific Triaminic formula."

Now let's perform the same examination of the **HOW** statement I've created here for Juicy Juice, again, in the context of a good *persuasive strategy*.

Juicy Juice

WHO: *A mom who wants her young children to get more nutrition*

WHAT: *100 percent pure juice that's healthful for your kids because it contains absolutely no added ingredients*

HOW: *Demonstrate that Juicy Juice is the healthy juice for kids by comparing its 100 percent pure juice–absolutely no added ingredients formulation with the ordinary competitive juice beverage drinks*

Let's also drill down into almost every word of the Juicy Juice **HOW**.

1. "Demonstrate that Juicy Juice is the healthy juice for kids" is action-oriented.

2. "Demonstrate" defines the specific action, because Mom must understand the difference that the product is offering to her.

3. "Comparing" vis-à-vis the competition is what the brand will actually do in its communications to its target customers.

4. "100 percent pure juice–absolutely no added ingredients" is honest. It's exactly what the product is and so it can easily deliver on the promise.

5. The *persuasive strategy* is tightly linked with the *core customer* "Mom" and the *uncommon offering* "100 percent pure juice . . . absolutely no added ingredients."

Honesty and Trust Create a Glittering Success

We've been focusing on the development of *persuasive strategies* for some mighty companies and brands. If your business is not in this stratosphere (not yet anyway) and you are wondering whether you really need to bother with this step in the Growth Discovery Process, I hope the following jewel of an entrepreneurial success story will inspire you to create a **HOW** for your business.

In the early years of the twentieth century, an emigrant from Eastern Europe found his way to a tiny oil-boom town in West Texas called Wichita Falls. His uncle offered him a small space in the back of his drugstore to sell his inexpensive jewelry. This highly entrepreneurial newcomer to America, Morris Zale, started selling the jewelry on credit (a radical new idea in the jewelry category) to the oilfield workers on their paydays. He built a reputation for honesty, and that reputation helped to build his business. Soon he opened his own small jewelry store down the street from the drugstore. That business grew, and in the 1930s he opened more credit jewelry stores in the new oil-boom towns of Oklahoma, West Texas, and the Gulf Coast of Texas.

When World War II began, Morris Zale expanded his rapidly growing enterprise into the towns around military bases in the Southwest and Midwest. The Zale family had a strong work ethic, an intimate knowledge of its customers, and a powerful offering—credit. As time went on, copycats emerged and credit became so abundant that this now-large chain of jewelry stores began searching for a new way to grow. In the mid-1970s, my father and I and our team at the agency helped Zales jewelers find that compelling new growth idea.

As you may have personally experienced when buying diamond jewelry, "trust" for your jeweler is a fundamental requirement because few of us have a clue about the cut, clarity, or value of a diamond. In the terms of my Growth Discovery Process, "trust" would become Zales's *uncommon offering*. But we needed to find a *persuasive strategy* that would cause the jewelry-buying public to go to Zales instead of the thousands of other jewelers in America.

Here is the *persuasive strategy* we created for Zales: *establish Zales as the trusted authority in diamonds by connecting the brand to diamonds.* You see, over time people have been conditioned to think of diamonds as the pinnacle of all jewelry, mainly due to the smart marketing efforts of the diamond industry's now-famous phrase "A Diamond is Forever." Unlike De Beers, the giant South African diamond mining company that coined that phrase, Zales stores feature a complete assortment of jewelry—other precious stones, pearls, gold and silver jewelry, and the like. We knew from experience that you stand for nothing if you try to stand for everything, so we decided to construct a very sturdy "small table" on which Zales could stand alone.

By standing for diamonds, the Zales brand would, over time, become synonymous with the pinnacle of all jewelry and this would imply that Zales was the best place to go for all jewelry. We did this by creating our own now-famous phrase "Zales, The Diamond Store." It not only became Zales's tagline, it became the centerpiece of all Zales's communications about the brand—inside the stores as well as throughout the local communities in which the stores were located. Our positioning of Zales, as expressed in its tagline and its entire marketing communications program, helped Zales grow to be the largest jewelry store chain in North America. To this day, "Zales, The Diamond Store" remains the centerpiece of all Zales's communications.

BLOOM
ON
GROWTH

You stand for nothing if you try
to stand for everything.

Mapping Your Own Route to Growth

How would you like to be the company that supplies half of the car navigation devices bought in Europe and a quarter of those sold in the United States? If you were that company you'd be called TomTom. You would be a Dutch firm with sales in the $1.5 billion range, and you would be wildly successful because you chose to buck conventional wisdom and take a very different route than your competitors. According to Harold Goddijn, CEO of TomTom and one of its four founders, as quoted in the *Financial Times*, his firm was the first company "to give car navigation consumer positioning, simplicity, style, and for acceptable mass-market prices." This is a terrific *uncommon offering* coupled with a *persuasive strategy* that promises ease of installation and ease of use, and it's all aimed at the consumer/user as *core customer*, not the auto industry. Goddijn states: "If we had followed conventional wisdom we would have tried to sell to the motor industry instead of the consumer electronics industry, and we would have failed." But the company didn't fail—it stood out by standing alone, and in 2006 it sold as many as 3.9 million route finders.

I was struck by TomTom's brief and lucid explanation of "what we do" on its Web site: "Today the company helps people get from A to B in 16 countries." Its unconventional stance is reflected in a simple, witty, and seemingly heartfelt wish for its customers, again from the Web site: "We hope you find happiness and fulfillment, as well as your destination."

Here's a very different illustration of standing alone on a small, sturdy strategic platform—and in a supposed commodity business to boot. On the face of it, nothing can be more commonplace or undistinguishable than a pencil. Yet Faber-Castell, the venerable pencil manufacturer founded over two hundred years ago, is, by design, in a class by itself. *The Economist* quotes the company's leader, Count Anton Wolfgang von Faber-Castell, as saying "we stuck with what we're good at," rather then attempting to fit itself into the digital world, as the company's consultants had advised. Instead, they worked to achieve the highest possible quality in their products, sustain the superb reputation they had earned over the centuries (*The Economist* offers a line of praise for their pencils from Vincent van Gogh: "They produce a capital black and are most agreeable for large studies"), and move into high-priced, high-design writing instruments. The idea of doing what you're good at and doing it better than anyone else is a key to developing an Inside Advantage.

Although I've never met Count Faber-Castell, I believe his **HOW**—his *persuasive strategy*—is most certainly focused on maintaining the quality of his premium products and letting customers and potential customers know that they are writing with one of the best pens or pencils in the world. The strategy is succeeding. According to *The Economist*, the company now makes two billion pencils a year, with sales of $530 million, and has factories at 16 sites worldwide. As for quality, in 2005, the count tossed 144 pencils out of the tower of his castle and "not one of them broke."

BLOOM ON GROWTH	Doing what you're good at and doing it better than anyone else is a key to developing an Inside Advantage.

Here's one additional story that shows how to stand out and away from the crowd. It describes the birth and growth of a now exceptionally successful company founded by a determined and talented entrepreneur I first met in the early 1980s. Our agency was working for a small, struggling client who owned but wasn't exploiting an exceptionally valuable asset with explosive potential—an 800 number.

To be specific, it was 1-800-FLOWERS. The magic of this number is that it immediately sets the owner apart and above every other flower vendor in the world. The number is so easy to remember that it is quickly recalled by any potential customer contemplating sending some flowers for an anniversary, birthday, or other personal or business reason.

I got a call from a man named Jim McCann who said he had come down to Dallas from New York to meet with me, knowing I had a client relationship with the owner of the number. Jim was a soft-spoken entrepreneur who owned some flower shops in the New York metropolitan area. I liked him a lot because he was sincere and seemed to understand the value of 1-800-FLOWERS. He wanted to know about our involvement with the company that owned it and said he was trying to buy it. As I recall, this transaction took a very long time. Jim was persistent and patient, and we kept in touch from time to time. In 1986 Jim said that he'd completed the purchase of the phone number and was going to study how to best grow with it. He did just that, and of course his success is the stuff of legend. In 2006, his company, listed on the Nasdaq stock exchange, had revenues of $781 million! Today, customers can purchase products by calling the now-famous number 24 hours a day, 7 days a week. Or they can buy online from 1-800-flowers.com, visit its 15 company-owned or 85 franchised stores, or go through its network of approximately 9,000 florists around the country.

My agency never had the opportunity to work with Jim directly; nonetheless, I've always admired his entrepreneurial instincts and the way he grew his company by standing out from the crowd and building a platform built for one on a telephone number: 1-800-FLOWERS.

I hope you're persuaded that my belief in that small, sturdy table built for one—standing alone and apart from the competition—is where you want to be with your business. In the next chapter we'll explore how to craft the *persuasive strategy* for your business, the blueprint you'll need to build that table.

CHAPTER 9

Create a Compelling Persuasive Strategy

Before we start developing the particular strategy you will use in your business to convince your *core customer* to buy your *uncommon offering*, I'd like to remind you why this effort is so worthwhile. Here are two quite different tales that emphasize the same point—getting it right in business beats the alternative.

The *Wall Street Journal* reported that restructuring costs through 2007 at the iconic Eastman Kodak Company "will total $3.6 billion to $3.8 billion" and "layoffs during the restructuring will total as many as 30,000 people."

And the *Financial Times* described a much smaller, but equally devastating financial and human outcome in its story about the failure of a promising Internet start-up. "That Art Site, an online business selling paintings and sculptures, lasted only nine months before it collapsed in debt. The founder even had to sell his house to cover the business's debts." While these two enterprises are different from each other in every way, they are exactly the same in this way: neither firm created an enduring *persuasive strategy*.

<table>
<tr><td>**BLOOM ON GROWTH**</td><td>Getting it right in business beats the alternative.</td></tr>
</table>

In this chapter we'll continue our journey toward getting it right by working together to develop a *persuasive strategy* for your business.

As in previous chapters when I showed you how to craft your **WHO** and **WHAT** statements, I will provide numerous examples of *persuasive strategies* developed with and for my consulting practice. Using the techniques in this chapter, I've been able to set apart enterprises of all sizes and types, even companies whose benefits are hard to imagine: A renowned symphony orchestra found its *persuasive strategy* in the promise that its musicians would deliver *visceral audience involvement in every performance*. A start-up fitness center promised that it would provide *a system of measurement that assures progress toward an individual's evolving health and fitness goals*.

You know that **HOW** is all about growing by persuading customers to buy your products or services, not your competitors'. Now you want to know how to construct one for your business. To get us started, we'll once again go behind the scenes of a real consulting session where the participants are eager to nail the third component in my Growth Discovery Process.

This company is a sizable West Coast golf products retail chain. Its goal, no surprise, is to accelerate its growth.

The company sells through two channels: large stores in or near malls and interactive marketing. It is growing, but not fast enough for its impatient investors. Stores represent the highest volume and interactive is the fastest growing—the channel with potential for even higher margins.

Each channel is managed by a fiercely competitive, independent team that reports to the president. It soon became obvious to me that this structure with two almost autonomous channels is a significant barrier to the growth of the business. To grow at the rate its investors aspire to, this firm would need to achieve total synergy among both channels. That means that each of the two channels must enthusiastically embrace the same *uncommon offering*. "Fat chance," I think, as I begin the session. Please see "A Bob Bloom Consulting Session—Finding Our **HOW**," which follows.

A BOB BLOOM CONSULTING SESSION

Finding Our HOW

I've been working most of the morning with the 10 or so senior executives who represent both channels, along with their corporate staff. We've been crafting their **WHO** and **WHAT** statements. It's been a tough day for everyone in the room because it's become painfully obvious that they have no appetite for a shared offering. But we have accomplished a lot.

We've determined that the target customer is, of course, a "golfer." In what seemed like seconds, they make clear that they want a particular golfer: one with money to spend on his or her addiction, as they call it, to the game. We quickly capture this objective in first few words of **WHO** on our chart: *An affluent, avid golfer*.

We then generate words and phrases that characterize this golfer's ultimate aspirations—words like *winning, competitive experience*, and *camaraderie*. Not being a golfer, I assume that avid golfers are single-minded about one thing—winning. However, I quickly learn that an avid golfer has less interest in winning and more interest in how he or she looks and feels when playing. So, oddly enough, consensus soon emerges for *a better golfing experience* rather than a *winning* experience. We all agree on this *core customer* statement:

WHO: *An affluent, avid golfer who constantly seeks a better golfing experience*

The discussion about **WHAT**—the company's *uncommon offering*—is far more challenging. We fill chart after chart with words such as *solutions, help, clubs, assistance, outfits, gear, products,* and *advice.* There is considerable discussion and considerable disagreement. I urge them to move beyond the products they sell, explaining that every one of their competitors sells clubs, balls, gear, and golfing attire.

The discussion gets far more complex. In the company's stores, they have golfing experts who provide advice to customers. This is a great *uncommon offering.* But the interactive people say that that offering is not possible on their Web site, their primary method of communicating with customers. The CEO, who knows that synergy among both channels offers vast growth potential as well as better margins, pushes back. He suggests that the Web site pages can be modified to incorporate the common graphics and verbiage that will emerge and to encourage customer input on their needs, problems, desires, and questions. He admits that this effort would require imagination, intense planning, changes in the order forms on the Web pages, close cooperation among the two channels, and considerable investment. He states quite firmly that the benefits of an *uncommon offering* like this could be huge because it would build a massive database of information on customer preferences. After much resistance from the interactive folks, there is (reluctant) agreement on the first few words of **WHAT**: *expert advice, customized assistance . . .* This is a victory for the CEO and is real breakthrough because the word *customized* is a very valuable concept.

We move on to the remainder of our statement. I ask the participants to create an image in their heads of their most important customer. I then ask them to describe how we can deliver the new service-oriented offering we've been discussing in a way that will resonate with our customer—that is, a way that will reflect that we share their intense desire for a "better golfing experience."

Meaningful and vivid words are called out: *enthusiasm, zeal, burning desire*, and finally, the word that everyone instantly falls for—*passion*. I don't want to risk this moment of agreement and quickly ask them "passion for what?" Someone yells "passion for the game." We finally have the emotional element we need to create an *uncommon offering*:

WHAT: *Expert advice, customized assistance, and a passion for helping our clients improve their game*

We take a needed break and come back for what I think will be a long, tough afternoon session.

So as soon as we begin, I'm delighted as *help golfing enthusiasts* emerges quickly as the opening words of the **HOW** statement without any other options offered. I am also pleased that his statement begins with a meaningful active verb that will energize their *persuasive strategy*. Then, *achieve their individual goals* flows from it with incredible ease. The *core customer* and *uncommon offering* are so specific, articulate, and meaningful that a wonderfully brief **HOW** almost writes itself:

HOW: *Help golfing enthusiasts achieve their individual goals*

I know from experience that this kind of sudden group agreement on **HOW** does occasionally occur, most often when there has been vigorous give and take and intense debate in the **WHO** and **WHAT** sessions. So when that particular pattern emerges, I'm not too surprised by it nor am I suspicious of the resulting **HOW** statement. Of course, we take the time to see that the first three components of the company's Growth Discovery Process fit snugly together. We are all reassured by what we see:

WHO: *An affluent, avid golfer who constantly seeks a better golfing experience*

> **WHAT:** *Expert advice, customized assistance, and a passion for helping our clients improve their game*
>
> **HOW:** *Help golfing enthusiasts achieve their individual goals*
>
> When this part of the session ends, everyone is exhausted but very pleased with the *persuasive strategy* we've created. However, I can't help but notice that the members of the interactive team now realize what they are facing: many months of hard work to implement this strategy in their channel. They don't yet realize that the reminder of our session devoted to **OWN IT!** will inspire their channel as well as the store channel with ideas, enthusiasm, and tactics toward their common goal of identifying and leveraging their company's Inside Advantage.

Finding Your HOW

Here are the steps that will help you to develop your *persuasive strategy* and turn it into a crisp, powerful **HOW** statement.

1. Begin by reviewing Part 3 of the book to refresh your memory and identify any questions that come to mind.

2. Don't try to draft your *persuasive strategy* yet. Instead, put your *core customer* and *uncommon offering* statements right in front of you. Please keep them there. They will reinforce the strategic path you have been on and highlight the path on which you will continue. Moreover, they will inspire you to think about **HOW** in the context of your Inside Advantage.

3. Look at each and every word of the first two components in your Growth Discovery Process. Sometimes, this undertaking can take a moment for you to tweak a word or two in either or both your *core customer* and *uncommon offering* statements. Try to avoid using the same word more than once in any component; this effort is not about form, it's about clarity. Different words can add fresh vitality to the statements. By this point, resist the temptation to make radical change unless they are absolutely essential. If you are working in a group, make sure you have total consensus for any and all changes. Continue to study these two statements because they are the key to **HOW**. After all, the exclusive purpose your *persuasive strategy* is to facilitate the sale of your **WHAT** to your **WHO**. Start thinking about the words or phrases or ideas that might be the right way to craft your **HOW**.

4. If you've done a truly great job on **WHO** and **WHAT**, the idea for **HOW** may become apparent very quickly, as it did for the West Coast golf products retail chain. But if it does take a while to emerge, just keep generating options. That's the road to a meaningful definition of **HOW** or any statement in the Growth Discovery Process—options and more options will produce a positive solution.

Ultimately, you'll spot an idea, word, or phrase that can be transformed into a strong *persuasive strategy*. Whether the idea jumps out quickly or slowly, put it to two tests: (1) Is it an idea that will enable you to sell your to your **WHAT** to your **WHO**? If it meets this essential hurdle, move to the second test. If it doesn't, come up with more options. (2) Ask the participant in the room who is responsible for sales in your company whether he or she feels "very confident" that this potential strategy will work. You're looking for an honest and definitive response. Whether the answer is yes or no, ask him or her why. Make sure that you and the rest of the group agrees. If the answer is "just maybe," immediately start generating more options. If you're a one-person company, switch gears and answer this vitally important question as honestly as you would expect your head of sales to. If you hit a brick wall, take a break. Getting away from any task often inspires results.

When you find the idea, word, or phrase that you and the group are excited about, compare it to all the others on the charts. If it still stands out, you probably have the central persuasive idea for your **HOW** statement.

5. **HOW** is all about taking some kind of action—an action that will connect **WHAT** and **WHO**. Thus, every **HOW** statement must begin with an active verb such as *own, capture, give, originate, create, transform, establish*, or *demonstrate*. You'll want to find the appropriate active verb to invigorate the central idea on which you've settled.

6. Before proceeding, take a close look at the **HOW** statements that follow. Each begins with an active verb and all have a powerful central idea that's been transformed into an actionable, aggressive *persuasive strategy*. Remember, they're here only for instruction and inspiration.

Core Customer WHO, WHAT, and HOW Statements

A National Chain of Suburban Newspapers

WHO: An active suburban homeowning family that cares about enhancing its quality of life and learning about local products and services that satisfy its needs and wants

WHAT: Timely, valuable news and information that touches the lives of the local community more consistently and comprehensively than any other source

HOW: Earn the community's trust and respect by helping to make it a better place to live

A West Coast Golf Products Retailer

WHO: An affluent, avid golfer who constantly seeks a better golfing experience

WHAT: Expert advice, customized assistance, and a passion for helping our clients improve their game

HOW: Help golfing enthusiasts achieve their individual goals

A Global Technology Provider

WHO: A global business enterprise that seeks the expert advice of a technology provider that understands its business

WHAT: A trusting partnership that ensures operational efficiency and valuable intelligence from its customers' technology investment

HOW: Earn a more intimate relationship by tailoring our services to our clients' ever-changing needs

A Renowned Symphony Orchestra

WHO: A frequent patron of classical music concerts who seeks a more passionate musical experience

WHAT: An orchestra that encourages every musician to share in the creation of an intensely memorable concert

HOW: Deliver visceral audience involvement in each concert

An Ultra-High-End Jewelry Store

WHO: An affluent local male or female status seeker who is looking for a fashion statement

WHAT: An incomparable selection of one-of-a-kind jewelry and watches offered in an elegant private setting

HOW: Create a reputation for an exclusive shopping and buying experience

A Start-Up Fitness Center

WHO: An adult man or woman who wants and can afford an exceptional personal training experience

WHAT: Consistent progress toward complete personal well-being, planned and monitored by expert trainers and nutritionists

HOW: Provide a system of measurement and expert advice that assures progress toward an individual's evolving health and fitness goals

A Prominent Wealth Management Firm

WHO: A prospective client with assets of $15+ million to invest plus an intense desire for special services and attention

WHAT: An expert financial advisor who delivers an unrivaled portfolio of customized services and exceptional investment results

HOW: Demonstrate the value of our services to clients and those that influence them to earn their loyalty and advocacy with prospective clients

An Upscale Chain of Tanning Salons

WHO: An image-conscious single woman who wants to look and feel better with little investment in time or money

WHAT: A tanning experience that exceeds customer expectations regarding amenities, privacy, and price

HOW: Invite tanners to experience our unique tanning salon without cost or obligation

A Sports and Entertainment Marketing Agency

WHO: A powerful marketer with a big ad budget that demands results-driven sponsorship programs

WHAT: Transfer the excitement, positive values, and dynamic imagery of sports and entertainment to brands

HOW: Take brands places they have never been and prove that we deliver results

A Publisher of Insurance Industry Data, News, and Other Information

WHO: A financial professional who provides advice and solutions to clients who want or need to be better informed about insurance

WHAT: The insurance industry's authoritative and comprehensive source of information, data, and analysis

HOW: Make our products and services indispensable to daily decision making

A Not-for-Profit Social Services Organization

WHO: An individual, a family, or a community that is underserved in terms of urgent human needs and lack of resources

WHAT: An organization dedicated to meeting the evolving health, living, and nutritional needs of the underserved in our community

HOW: Conduct and publish a comprehensive survey of our community's changing needs every two years

When you start writing your *persuasive strategy*, remember, you want no more than 10 to 15 words, and **HOW** statements are often shorter. But whatever the length, each word must have meaning and help you to define **HOW** you are going to sell **WHAT** to **WHO**. Keep the words directly related to your *core customer* and *uncommon offering*, and find fresh new words that are not utilized in the first two components.

As always, examine your **HOW** one more time to assure it's as good as you can make it. Again, ask yourself whether it will enable you to sell your **WHAT** to your **WHO**. Put the three components of your Growth Discovery Process on the same page or chart, and verify that there is complete linkage. This step is essential to your growth objective; take some time to assure that there is complete integration of these strategic elements. When you're sure that the first three components of your Growth Discovery Process work in complete harmony, you are ready to create the *imaginative acts* that will release your Inside Advantage.

The Inside Advantage FAQ—HOW

You may have some questions about **HOW**. If so, please review the frequently asked questions that follow.

Q: How can you tell if a strategy is persuasive?

A: First, ask yourself if the strategy, as written, is really credible: do you believe it? That's the first test. Next, ask yourself this question: would this motivate me to buy the product or service? Of course, you may not be the *core customer*, but you can try to put yourself in that person's shoes. Or you can talk to some people who actually live in those shoes and ask them the same question. The answers will help you decide if the strategy is truly persuasive.

Q: How would you define *strategy* and *tactic*?

A: There are always many definitions of every term, including *strategy* and *tactic*. Definition isn't too important. Rather than definition, let's concentrate on understanding the practical application of these terms—a strategy says *how* you intend to achieve your goal; a tactic is the *way* you intend to implement your strategy.

Q: How can I tell if my **HOW** is good enough to lock it in?

A: Locking in is not the goal—stay flexible. I often find a word or two I want to tweak days, months, or even years after I create one. Time changes or I gain perspective or something just sounds better or works better. Words are important, but words can be improved or moved around. The fundamental issue is whether **HOW** can sell the **WHAT** to **WHO**. Lock it down only when you're confident it will move your sales needle.

Q: When will I understand "how" to put my **HOW** to work to grow my business?

A: You probably have already thought of some ways to put it work. But, I suggest that you just capture those ideas for the moment. Wait until you discover **OWN IT!** in the next part of the book—then you'll see how to make full use of your imagination.

Q: Please explain how emotion ties into **HOW**.

A: The customer's emotion(s) is the most central aspect of selling. We're simply trying to sell something to that customer by understanding his or her emotions. That's why we must always keep emotions in mind. You know that your *core customer* has emotions because, like you and me, he or she is a human being. You know that your *uncommon offering* must deliver both a tangible benefit and an emotional benefit to the customer because that's how she or he will make a purchase decision. That means that your *persuasive strategy* must be linked to the emotional aspects of **WHO** and **WHAT**.

The first three components of the Growth Discovery Process are the strategic foundation of your Inside Advantage. The fourth and final component is the magical way you will put your *persuasive strategy* to work—the way you can make your *uncommon offering* well known to your *core customer*, and make full use of your Inside Advantage.

I'll open the door to **OWN IT!** in the next and last part of the book—all you have to do is open the door to your imagination.

Imaginative
Acts

CHAPTER 10

Never Stop Celebrating Your Advantage

Your highly motivating **WHO**, **WHAT**, and **HOW** will be defined in the privacy of your office or conference room. The strategic framework that will come out of this process will be sound and smart, but it will still be a secret, known only to the few people who participated in the process. It's not yet an Inside Advantage because potential customers are not aware of it, not curious about it, not captivated by it, and not drawn to it.

Worse! They don't even know that the compelling customer benefits you've defined belong to your business and not to your competitors'. You don't yet **OWN IT!** But you will soon—that's what this chapter will show you how to do. Once you **OWN IT!** your business will start growing.

The final component in the Growth Discovery Process will enable you to **OWN IT!** by making your *uncommon offering* well known to your *core customer*. In the next few pages you will discover how easy and fun it can be to create a series of *imaginative acts* that will celebrate your *uncommon offering* and link it inextricably to your business. When this happens, you will unlock your Inside Advantage and grow your business. The magical moment in your business is when customers decide to buy your product or service and not your competitors'.

This is the very moment that customers experience your Inside Advantage. **OWN IT!** makes this magical moment happen by bringing your strategy to life with a series of *imaginative acts*. This is how **OWN IT!** fits in the Growth Discovery Process:

WHO + WHAT + HOW + OWN IT! = INSIDE ADVANTAGE

WHO is the *core customer* most likely to buy your product or service in the quantity required for optimal profit.

WHAT is the *uncommon offering* that your business will own and leverage.

HOW is the *persuasive strategy* that will convince your *core customer* to buy your *uncommon offering* versus all competitive offerings.

OWN IT! is the series of *imaginative acts* that will celebrate your *uncommon offering* and make it well known to your *core customer*.

Here's how **OWN IT!** works in the marketplace: people are intrigued and motivated by *imaginative acts* because they highlight and dramatize the Inside Advantage of businesses and brands.

Like all things original, innovative, and yes, magical, *imaginative acts* must be experienced. So sit back and enjoy the many illustrations of businesses, big and small, that have grown with **OWN IT!** Then you'll be eager to discover how to create a series of *imaginative acts* for your business whether you have a big budget or none at all.

> The magical moment in your business is when customers decide to buy your product or service and not your competitors'.

Inventing Imaginative Acts

This example of the creation and execution of a series of *imaginative acts* in support of a product also happens to be the project that first inspired me to develop and give voice to the concept of **OWN IT!**

One day my agency received a call from our large client, Sandoz (now Novartis). The Swiss pharmaceutical giant wanted to reward us for our performances on its Triaminic and Theraflu brands by giving us an even more challenging assignment. Its CEO explained that Tavist, its highly successful prescription drug product used to treat severe cold and allergy symptoms, had just received approval by the Food and Drug Administration (FDA) for conversion to an over-the-counter (OTC) medicine. That meant that the brand could be sold in drugstores, supermarkets, and convenience stores.

The client had the strategic framework and packaging ready to go and wanted to mount a significant media campaign to announce that Tavist could now be purchased without prescription. From previous experience with conversions from prescription to over-the-counter (Rx-to-OTC) medication we understood the challenge: when a medicine becomes available over the counter, its formerly loyal users perceive it to be less efficacious, and potential new customers, as yet unfamiliar with the brand and its therapeutic benefits, and not trusting it, are reluctant to give it a try. However, we had plenty of time and moved forward with development of advertising.

Up jumped the devil. The FDA unexpectedly and inexplicably modified one element of Tavist's official "monograph," the product's treatment protocol and efficacy. In simple terms, this meant that there could be no reference of any kind to the treatment of colds—it had to be marketed as a product for severe nasal congestion only! We were suddenly faced with two huge obstacles: we had a much smaller *core customer* base, given that we couldn't talk directly to the big cold sufferers market, and we had a weaker offering—the relief of severe nasal congestion rather than relief from all the symptoms of a bad cold such as headache, coughing, and sneezing. And enough time had passed that we no longer had the luxury of a far-off deadline. We had to move, and fast.

The client concentrated on packaging changes and launch details; we were given the task of developing a blockbuster introductory campaign concurrent with the launch date now just around the corner. Given the set of obstacles that confronted us and the approaching deadline, I assembled a large group of specialists—media, public relations, writing and art talent, promotion experts, and the like—from all our U.S. offices. We quickly concluded that traditional media advertising would be insufficient to generate the consumer awareness and customer trial required. We needed something even bigger—something that would generate national impact and motivate potential customers to give the OTC version of Tavist an immediate try.

It was then that I remembered a remarkable event-driven concept developed by Marc Bourgery, an agency colleague in our Paris headquarters. Marc and I had worked together on client and new business opportunities in Europe. I thought him to be the most unorthodox and innovative strategist I had ever worked with. I had seen Marc's concept produce the kind of impact and urgency we needed for Tavist. The event I witnessed firsthand was the introduction of a new fragrance brand that needed instant fanfare, notoriety, and press coverage. The product's point of difference was its floral scent. Marc's concept was put into action. On the morning of the brand's introduction, Paris awakened to discover that several of the famous bridges over the Seine River were covered entirely with the flowers that created this scent. Paris was awed by this audacious event and the impact was immediate and enormous. If a single act could produce this kind of result, I thought, multiple *imaginative acts* would produce even greater impact. This was the inspiration for **OWN IT!**—the fourth component of the Growth Discovery Process that you'll use to unlock your Inside Advantage.

Trying to find a solution to the Tavist crisis, I described this event and its enormous impact to our agency specialists assembled in New York. They had little faith in such an unconventional approach, but no one had a better idea, so we moved forward along this path. We worked hard, fast, and harmoniously because we had no choice.

We discussed the potential customer we could talk to as well the one we could not talk to directly due to FDA restrictions. We agreed the two customers were one and the same, even though we couldn't use the word *cold*. Here's how we defined our *core customer*:

WHO: *An adult suffering from severe nasal congestion, regardless of the cause*

We identified the brand's inherent customer benefit—its prescription heritage—and due to the FDA restrictions, this benefit became the foundation of our *uncommon offering*:

WHAT: *A powerful new over-the-counter medicine with a well-regarded prescription drug heritage for the relief of severe nasal congestion*

We agreed on the *persuasive strategy*:

HOW: *Exploit the product's well-known prescription drug heritage to reassure current users and generate trial from those who suffer from severe cold and allergy symptoms*

Now we needed a compelling series of *imaginative acts* to assure that the launch was a huge success, and we needed to create these tactics by the end of our work session.

For well over an hour, many ideas were generated. All were either impractical or impotent. Finally, one of our creative stars said something like this: "Let's just tell our potential customers that, as of the launch date, they can 'breathe easier.'" This two-word expression *breathe easier* was the genesis of an amazing success story and made drug history.

We turned our attention to creating *imaginative acts* to communicate this profoundly simple expression. I explained that we were looking for a giant "coat rack" on which we could hang all our *imaginative acts*. Our brightest PR professional gave us that "coat rack"—she said, "Let's announce that our launch day will be 'Breathe Easier America Day.'" In effect, we were creating a new "American holiday" to celebrate a now easily obtainable remedy for people with stopped-up noses! We now had an astonishingly imaginative idea that would make Tavist's Inside Advantage a well-known reality.

And the ideas, ubiquitous and explosive, flowed and soon became reality. Inexpensive and quick-to-produce network TV ads announced the "breaking news" with crawlers across the screen: "Seven days before Breathe Easier America Day," then "Six days before Breathe Easier America Day," and so on until we announced "Breathe Easier America Day is here!" with the news that the prescription drug Tavist was now available over the counter. Press releases were sent to big and small newspapers alike; a well-trained "Breathe Easier America" spokesperson appeared on radio news shows and early-morning network TV shows; and point-of-purchase signs were placed on drugstore shelves to tell customers that Tavist would help them "breathe easier." There were numerous other *imaginative acts* that celebrated the brand's OTC launch, but there was never a mention of "colds," and all acts were built on the sound strategic foundation we had enunciated.

The Tavist launch was, in fact, an enormous success. Overnight the little-known prescription brand name became well known as an over-the-counter product. Sales were higher than expected. The buzz was everywhere. One of the drug trade magazines called it the most successful Rx-to-OTC conversion since Tylenol. It was a testimony to the process that is the focus of this chapter: **OWN IT!**

The Most Lavish Imaginative Acts

Stanley Marcus, the great retailer and marketing genius, created an amazing series of *imaginative acts*—very likely the most lavish ever conceived and executed. His *imaginative acts* are the renowned Neiman Marcus "French Fortnight" celebrations.

Earlier in the book we examined the promotions designed to stimulate sales during Neiman Marcus's mid-October slow selling season. These Fortnight events are the result of Stanley's ingenuity and matchless understanding of the role of theater in the world of fashion.

While he didn't use my process to come up with the kind of *imaginative acts* that Fortnight represents, he did understand instinctively that his store represented something special and uncommon. In a speech to British, French, and Italian manufacturing groups, he urged them not only to learn the differences between European and American markets and the differing markets within the United States, but also "why a Neiman Marcus is different from a Macy's." Stanley understood the value of his Inside Advantage.

If I could have had the privilege to work through the Growth Discovery Process with Stanley Marcus, we probably would have come up with something like this to represent the **WHO**, **WHAT**, and **HOW** elements of the famous Neiman Marcus Fortnights:

WHO: *Upscale fashion-conscious man or woman who lives in or near Dallas or travels to it*

WHAT: *The arbiter of fashion in America*

HOW: *Honor a particular nation's culture, distinctive traditions, craftsmanship, and fashion in a 14-day October event that will captivate our clientele, create festive occasions that require chic attire, and generate acclaim for our brand*

The very first Fortnight—the famous French Fortnight—took place in October 1957. Here is a glimpse of what made this extraordinary series of *imaginative acts* so effective and so memorable. Details are taken from Stanley Marcus's memoir, *Minding the Store*.

To gain the involvement of the entire Dallas community, Stanley invited "the presidents of all the luncheon clubs; the directors of the museums, the orchestra, the theater; the heads of the schools; the mayor; and everybody else who might conceivably participate."

The result of this initiative was the transformation of an entire city deep in the heart of Texas into a celebration of a foreign country called France—and a purely commercial event called the Neiman Marcus French Fortnight.

Envision this series of *imaginative acts* funded, not by Neiman Marcus, but by civic institutions, charities, French firms, and private associations: an exhibition of never-before-shown-in-America Toulouse-Lautrec paintings at the Dallas Museum; the largest exhibition of French tapestries ever shown in the United States at the Dallas municipal auditorium; prominent French speakers at numerous luncheon clubs; a gala charity ball in honor of the ambassador from France; and an Air France plane full of French dignitaries, celebrities, and fashion gurus. And these are just a few of the unprecedented activities.

Stanley proudly described the ribbon cutting at the store in this way: "The façade of our building . . . had been transformed to resemble the boutiques of the Faubourg St. Honoré . . . our first floor decorated with huge photo-murals depicting the Place de la

Concorde . . . white Renaults in the aisles." French manufacturers, designers, and craftspeople exhibited their fashionable goods and couture merchandise throughout the store.

Here's the way Stanley expressed the results of the French Fortnight: "We accomplished our objective of enlarging business during a period of passive customer interest. We turned October into a month of peak traffic, even surpassing Christmas; we attracted thousands of new customers to the store and we enhanced our national and international reputation."

What Stanley Marcus accomplished is a triumphant marriage of both strategy and imagination. He celebrated his store's Inside Advantage in a manner that most likely will never duplicated. His Fortnights helped propel Neiman Marcus into the forefront of fashion retailers, and they brought the company worldwide renown.

Coolest Imaginative Acts

Like Stanley Marcus with his store, Steve Jobs has an instinctive understanding of the essential need for Apple to stand alone—to avoid competing head to head with brands that have more muscle or that can be produced for a lower price point.

Jobs has developed a strategic framework to keep Apple's products distinctive and different and to keep his company one or more steps ahead of the competition.

Also like Marcus, Jobs and Apple have employed many *imaginative acts* to create an iconic image for his brand.

> **BLOOM ON GROWTH**
> Avoid competing head to head with brands that have more muscle or that can be produced for a lower price point.

One of the most famous of Apple's *imaginative acts* was the Super Bowl commercial that introduced Apple's Macintosh computer in January 1984. Directed by noted filmmaker Ridley Scott, the ad represented Apple and its products as being different, more alive, more colorful—sexier—than competitors who were represented by bald-headed drones in a gray Orwellian world being addressed by Big Brother. Apple was creating a different table to stand on, one that would hold only them and would most purposely exclude Bill Gates's Microsoft. Apple was going to be different and was going to make the world different. As the announcer intoned that with the introduction of the Mac, "1984 will not be like '1984.'"

Fast-forward 20 years. Jobs's legendary annual MacWorld keynote address is eagerly awaited by the entire high-tech world. In 2007, for example, he introduced Apple's impressive new iPhone, wowing the crowd as he demonstrated its many impressive features, including video and audio streaming capabilities.

Here's Jobs's brilliant strategy: he invents small, cool-looking, innovative electronic devices or none at all. He never deviates. He always breaks new ground. He never comes out with a me-too product or a mere gimmick or anything without a tangible and emotional benefit. But—and here's the most brilliant concept of all—he always focuses exclusively on the products' emotional benefits, not the tangible benefits.

Year after year, Jobs's brilliant way to **OWN IT!** is to have his admirers, the press, and yes, even his detractors and competitors wait for the familiar celebration of another groundbreaking new product—the Apple II, the Mac, the iPod, the iTunes Store, or the iPhone. He always celebrates his product's introduction in the same dramatic way. He never exaggerates or grandstands, but he always commands the spotlight and generates massive worldwide press. Time after time we see video clips and large photos of Jobs in his jeans and dark turtleneck shirt. In the palm of his hand, he's holding yet another very small, very sleek, very innovative new product for the world to see, adore, and buy. His may be the longest-running series of explosive *imaginative acts* ever. Each of them in turn reinforces the company's Inside Advantage.

Imaginative Acts Spring from Strategic Reality

Imaginative acts can be as elaborate as a nationwide promotion event, as simple as a personalized e-mail communication, or somewhere in between.

My client L'Oréal launched Garnier Fructis shampoo in 2003, quickly gaining share from Procter & Gamble with a national advertising campaign and a big attention-getting, press-generating event that celebrated the product's fresh and natural approach to hair care. The promotional event featured L'Oréal staffers driving around metropolitan areas in light green buses—the same color as Fructis shampoo bottles. They handed out samples of the new product along with literature describing its *uncommon offering*—its fresh and natural approach to hair care. The result was a lot of buzz, trial, and sales.

BLOOM ON GROWTH	*Imaginative acts* can be as elaborate as a nationwide promotion event, as simple as a personalized e-mail communication, or somewhere in between.

You'll remember Jack Mitchell from an earlier chapter. He's the owner of two remarkably successful specialty stores in Connecticut, Richards in Greenwich and Mitchells in Westport. In early January of every year I receive a personal e-mail from Jack thanking me for my patronage of his store and wishing me and my family a Happy New Year. This is not an appeal to buy anything—rather it's a no-cost way to celebrate with me Jack's caring, personalized service, the *uncommon offering* of his business. It's the way

Jack "hugs" his customers. Incidentally, Jack literally wrote the book on the subject of exceptional customer service, which he calls *Hug Your Customers*.

One of my clients, the publisher of financial data, is employing a comprehensive annual survey that will describe subscribers' views of financial industry trends in considerable detail. The publisher will release the survey with great fanfare on the opening day of its most important industry convention in order to dominate the show's news and press. This relevant, topical, and reliable data will celebrate the firm's *uncommon offering*—its authoritative position in the financial publishing industry.

In each of these examples, you can see how tightly a single *imaginative act* ties in to the business or brand's strategic framework: the colorful shampoo and literature giveaway ties in with the product's beneficial fruit concentrate ingredient, and, of course, puts the product in the hands of potential customers. Jack's e-mail to me reminds me of the highly personalized service his stores consistently offer customers. The financial industry survey proves and reinforces the publisher's authoritative approach to its financial products and services. These illustrations highlight just one of a series of *imaginative acts* conceived and implemented by these marketers. It's the cumulative impact of act after act after act that unleashes the Inside Advantage and enables a marketer to **OWN IT!**

A Nontraditional Method of Communication

OWN IT! is not about a tagline or a slogan. It's not about awareness building or brand building. It's an untraditional communications medium designed to work in today's complex and challenging world. In today's environment the expense of communicating effectively by traditional means can be virtually prohibitive.

The function of **OWN IT!** is to create *imaginative acts* that will celebrate your *uncommon offering* and link it inextricably to your business—to capitalize on your Inside Advantage. **OWN IT!** is driven by a strategic framework formed by **WHO, WHAT,** and **HOW** in the Growth Discovery Process.

Many business leaders, seasoned pros and struggling entrepreneurs alike, don't appear to understand or embrace the reality of today's marketplace or realize how cynical and jaded our society has become about slick slogans and over-the-top ad campaigns. When exposed to advertising bravado with such frequency, customers and potential customers simply turn off. I can't tell you how often I've heard heads of businesses describe their need to grow, not in the context of strategy, but in terms of the advertising they envision or the taglines they admire or want. I've heard: "We need a new approach to advertising" or "We need a great slogan like our big competitors" or "Nobody knows what we stand for so I want an awareness building marketing campaign with a great tagline." Such approaches are expensive and, more often than not, wrong-headed and ultimately ineffective.

> **BLOOM ON GROWTH**
>
> In today's environment, the expense of communicating effectively by traditional means can be virtually prohibitive.

They—and we—can learn a great deal by studying the way Southwest Airlines links *imaginative acts* to its brand. In 1971 we created a traditional airline schedule ad with an untraditional headline: "How Much Do We Love You? Let Us Count the Ways." Could this ad be owned by any airline other than Southwest? That's what linkage is all about. As Southwest was short of cash in the early years, we couldn't afford advertising that would plant a tagline or a slogan firmly in the minds of potential customers. Instead we put "love" into everything Southwest did: drinks were called Love

Potions, drink coupons were Love Stamps, peanuts became Love Bites, tickets were issued from Love Machines, and, yes, an airplane was called the Love Bird. Six years later we created an ad that heralded expansion to Texas cities other than the ones we already flew to: "We're Spreading Love All Over Texas." Had we left out the logo in the ad, everyone living in Texas at that time would have known whose ad it was. Most likely, everyone in the United States would know this today. That's what **OWN IT!** is all about.

Your *imaginative acts* will make your company well known — but not well known to the entire buying public and not well known for just anything (or everything). **OWN IT!** is efficient as well as effective because it focuses exclusively on your business's most potent inherent strategic assets. It celebrates your *uncommon offering* and, unlike traditional media, makes it well known to the audience most critical to your growth — your *customer* and *potential customer*. Unless you **OWN IT!**, even vast amounts of money devoted to marketing will prove to be impotent.

OWN IT! aggregates a series of *imaginative acts* to achieve cumulative impact. It's designed to be flexible, easy, quick to implement, and cost effective. Here's the most important point to keep in mind: **OWN IT!** is not about creating a collection of tactical market elements — it's about executing a program tightly integrated with your strategic framework as defined by the Growth Discovery Process.

BLOOM ON GROWTH   Unless you **OWN IT!**, even vast amounts of money devoted to marketing will prove to be impotent.

Many no- or low-cost *imaginative acts* can work together and stand alone. Or they can be combined with one or more of the traditional methods of communication to link the brand or company with its Inside Advantage; for example: public relations can be employed to reach a particular market segment, the Internet can be used to attract interested shoppers, or advertising can be employed to reach larger customer segments. Celebrating your company's Inside Advantage like this is the surest way to grow any size or type of business in today's costly, complex, and skeptical world.

Juicy Juice and Triaminic Unlock Their Inside Advantages

Throughout the book we've been documenting the discovery of the *core customer*, the *uncommon offering*, and the *persuasive strategies* of two highly successful brands—Juicy Juice and Triaminic. Let's now focus on just a few of the series of *imaginative acts* each brand employed to grow.

To **OWN IT!** Triaminic and our agency agreed that we needed to reinforce the brand's commitment to helping moms understand, diagnose, and treat their kids' minor health problems. The Triaminic product manager emphasized that the brand needed to be a real part of the solution, not just an advertiser selling a line of products that happened to be symptom-specific. Our advertising staff couldn't think outside the advertising box, so we called in our public relations specialists. They said the brand should provide valuable information and useful up-to-the-minute news that would assist moms with their challenging and stressful task. They recommended that we create a "Triaminic Parents Club." Members would receive a free quarterly online or offline newsletter with practical information relevant to the health and well-being of young children, timely bulletins about cold alerts by region, articles from medical journals about the danger of overmedicating young children and, of course, new product news and special offers about our line of symptom-specific products. Moms were invited to provide the names and addresses of their friends and neighbors. The Triaminic Parents Club was the centerpiece of the brand's series of *imaginative acts* that focused on its system-specific *uncommon offering*: it was promoted on the package and at point of sale, it was communicated to pharmacists and pediatricians, it was well publicized on leading TV and radio shows and in key magazines with mom audiences, and, of course, it was featured in the brand's magazine and network TV advertising directed at moms.

Juicy Juice's approach to **OWN IT!** also had to help moms, but in this instance, we had to be very careful not to "lecture" them about their role as a good mother. We needed to find someone to deliver our message to moms—someone they would listen to, believe, and, most of all, like. This ruled out other moms, authoritative spokespersons, and health-care experts. One of our creative directors, a mother of three small kids, gave us the perfect solution. She said: let's use charming kids in our TV advertising. This was, she said, the perfect way to inform moms about the health benefits afforded by Juicy Juice and to take the edge off the blunt comparison to competitive products that had sugar, coloring, and water as their main ingredients. Juicy Juice's *uncommon offering* became well known to moms through its kids-to-moms messaging and its numerous other *imaginative acts*. Juicy Juice was one of the first brands to sponsor the now exceptionally popular and well-respected *Arthur* animated TV program on PBS that premiered in 1996. The program targeted kids, but many moms were sitting with their kids to watch this more intelligent and socially responsible PBS show. The brand provided educational literature for pediatricians' offices. Juicy Juice used point of sale to highlight the benefits of its healthy ingredients, and there were frequent interviews and public relations features about the brand in magazines and on TV shows directed to moms. *Imaginative acts* about its *uncommon offering* communicated to the *core customer* enabled Juicy Juice to **OWN IT!**

Imaginative Acts for a Diverse Business

Now, let's once again go behind the scenes of a consulting session—this time to experience the development of **OWN IT!** The challenge here was to find one strategic framework and one series of *imaginative acts* that could be used by my client's numerous businesses located in different parts of the United States.

This company publishes local newspapers in numerous suburban communities located around sprawling metropolitan areas. To make the situation even more complex, each newspaper has a different name. It's a large, fast-growing firm that's very well managed, and it's riding the wave of U.S. exurban and suburban migration.

As this coherent strategic framework is so critical to the creation of our *imaginative acts*, we'll carefully review the development of **WHO, WHAT**, and **HOW** before moving on to **OWN IT!** Please see "A Bob Bloom Consulting Session—**OWN IT!**— Finding Our Imaginative Acts," which starts on the next page.

You've seen a lot in this chapter about celebrating your business's *uncommon offering* with **OWN IT!** And you've learned how a strategic framework sets up your capability to create *imaginative acts*. Perhaps you've begun to see ways that your own business can become well known to your *core customer* for your *uncommon offering* through a series of *imaginative acts*.

Before we start applying the **OWN IT!** part of the Growth Discovery Process to your business, let's examine the nature of *imaginative acts* themselves. You've noticed that we've made the distinction between small and large acts, and low- or no-cost acts and costly ones. There are reasons to use either or both, depending on the particulars of your business and your budget. Again, the smaller, easier, more common sort of *imaginative acts* I call *ubiquitous acts* and the larger, rarer kind I call *explosive acts*. The next chapter will show you how these acts complement and supplement each other and how they can be used to celebrate your Inside Advantage.

OWN IT!—Finding Our Imaginative Acts

The participants are indeed diverse: our session includes editorial, production, distribution, advertising sales, finance, and administration as well as top management. For almost all in attendance, this is their first exposure to growth strategy, so I'm thinking this could be an especially difficult experience for all us.

My normal setup of the Growth Discovery Process and our working procedures is met with stony silence—not a good sign. We're working in a long, narrow room, so I am having difficulty getting eye contact with those in the back. The development of options for our **WHO**—our *core customer*—is slow. The participants are interested, but they are reacting and responding rather stiffly and formally. I urge everyone to lighten up and get into the act.

The charts on my easels start to fill up with a wider and richer range of potential *core customers* for the company's newspapers: advertisers, municipal officials, homemakers, sports enthusiasts, homebuilders, retailers, families, car dealers, and so on. We fill chart after chart with names of potential *core customers*. I emphasize that we're looking for their single most important customer. Many resist the question, saying that they have a variety of customers and all are vital to the business's success. I once again explain the concept of a *core customer* and ask them to visualize this individual. This seems to help, and we begin to circle a shorter and better list of *core customer* options, but it becomes obvious that each participant is visualizing a different customer because of his or her functional position in the organization.

Finally, we narrow the *core customer* options to three: advertisers, municipal officials, and families. Trying to get to *the* customer who can drive their firm's growth, I ask them to identify the most important customer of both the municipal officials and the advertisers. They discuss this issue and come to agreement that it's a "home-owning family." They explain to me that a "homeowning family" consists of the people who buy the most goods and services and have the biggest stake in the community. I let them convince themselves that a "homeowning family" is their *core customer*. They are relieved and enthused, and so am I.

Then, I ask them to describe a "homeowning family" so we can complete our **WHO** statement. The advertising people in the room stress the obvious: this family buys the products and services that the newspapers' advertisers sell. The editorial people offer another perspective: this family reads the newspaper's community-focused stories to better understand the area from a quality-of-life perspective—that, after all, is why they moved to the suburbs and bought a home. We use both ideas in our *core customer* statement adding the word *active* because it characterizes the homeowners the newspapers' advertisers want to reach—people who buy cars, build swimming pools, and buy sports equipment. Our *core customer* is:

WHO: *An active suburban homeowning family that cares about enhancing its quality of life and learning about local products and services that satisfy its needs and wants*

The group comes back from our break very enthusiastic and ready to create its *uncommon offering*. With the rich *core customer* statement as a headlight, we generate some outstanding words and phrases describing what the participants believe they are giving their customers. There's a lot of good material here—this time with more quality than quantity—with people mentioning editorials, news, ads, updates, information, articles, sports results, and community problems and progress. Two words emerge, and both add real texture and substance: *timely* and *valuable*. We agree on *timely, valuable news and information* as the centerpiece of the **WHO** statement. That's the tangible benefit the company's newspapers deliver to the suburban homeowner, but where's the emotional benefit? We agree on the direction of this emotional benefit, but struggle to find the exact right words; eventually we do: *timely, valuable news and information that touches the lives of the local community*. Nice.

The group thinks we're finished, but I don't. I say this statement could describe any newspaper, radio, or TV station—what makes your "timely, valuable news and information" better or different? The editorial people come to the rescue with *more consistently and comprehensisvely than any other source*. It's meaningful, but I remind the editorial folks that they have just set a very high standard. They say they are up to it (I'll come back to this later). So now we have our *uncommon offering*:

WHAT: *Timely, valuable news and information that touches the lives of the local community more consistently and comprehensively than any other source*

We test the integration of **WHO** and **WHAT** and find that we have a sound logical fit. The key is our dedication to the people of the community, and a promise to understand what is important to them and to keep them informed about everything that they care about. The promise is a serious one, especially if the company is to do it better than any other news source in the community, including radio, television, and Internet.

We move on to **HOW**. Generating words and phrases isn't too productive. I just don't see anything worthwhile. Such lack of inspiration happens occasionally, and when it does, it's best to stop and have some dialogue centered on the components of the process that have just been completed. I push the group to define what the "active suburban homeowning family" wants for its community that we could own and leverage. The head of marketing says something very insightful: "these folks have moved to the suburbs to find a better place to live, and I think we help them do this better than the metropolitan newspapers, TV, and radio stations because we are the medium that is most involved in their community." The group loves this highly competitive idea, and we quickly agree that this could provide the "versus all competitive offerings" notion we need for our statement. We write: *helping to make the community a great place to live*. I ask the group *how* they do this, because this will define a *persuasive strategy*. One of the editorial staff says: "We earn the community's trust and respect." Before we complete our *persuasive strategy* I remind every participant that we are once again setting a very high performance standard. They all say they are up for it as written:

HOW: *Earn the community's trust and respect by helping to make it a better place to live*

I conclude this part of the meeting by congratulating the group on constructing a very sound strategic framework for their growth and ask them to come back from their break ready to generate many *imaginative acts* that will make their *uncommon offering* well known to their *core customer*.

Upon their return, I set up four separate breakout groups, making sure each one includes individuals from all the company's functional roles. This is my way of ensuring interaction within the group. The task, I remind them, is to generate a long list of *imaginative acts* focused on making their **WHAT** well known to their **WHO**. They go off to their assigned corners of the big room with their easels and markers.

It looks to me like they are having a terrific time—shouting out ideas and clapping and booing each other's contributions. They're

jotting down a host of ideas, some that prove to be very imaginative, some that are very ordinary, and a lot that duplicate the lists of
the other groups.

In about 45 minutes we reconvene as a large group, and a
spokesperson for each group takes us rapidly through their ideas
amidst more cheering, clapping, and booing. Together we eliminate
the duplicates and circle the remaining acts that appear to offer
the most promise. Many are editorial ideas; some are community
events they can sponsor; some are graphic and visual ways to own
and leverage their passionate commitment to the community;
some are ways to curry the favor of the municipal officials or the
sports-minded, religious-minded, civic-minded, and cultural-
minded citizens; some ideas relate to schools and religious institutions; others tie to local athletic teams, annual community events,
and celebrations.

Over 150 possible *imaginative acts* are generated in less than an
hour. Here's a sampling:

• Reader coffee talks with reporters

• Reader feedback panel

• Cheer cards to hospital patients

• Free article lamination service

• Advertiser appreciation lunches

• "Where are they now?" stories about local high school grads

• Recipe contests

• Community calendar

• Sponsorship of the annual Fourth of July celebration

- Amateur art contests

- Putting a phrase like "Helping You Build a Better (Town Name)" on the masthead of the paper, delivery cars, business cards, telephone greeting, banners for community events

- New-neighbor showcase

- Creation of a community spirit award

- Sponsorship of a food drive or a holiday toy drive

- Sponsorship of a community Special Olympics program

All the participants are proud of their collective efforts. All pledge that when they return to their home offices around the country that they will work with the local staff of their newspaper to choose and launch a series of *imaginative acts* from among the ones we have generated appropriate to their community.

I congratulate the entire group for establishing a sound strategic framework and generating such a large and rich list of *imaginative acts* from which the local papers can draw. Someone asks how they should select which acts to implement and whether they all have to be implemented simultaneously. I explain that all acts do not have to be executed at the same moment but that they will optimize awareness and drama by performing them as a series of acts and as closely together as possible. Then I offer these guidelines for selecting among and organizing the many acts: consistency with the *persuasive strategy*, bang for the buck, ease and speed of execution, and anticipated result.

Additionally, I urge that each newspaper divide its acts into two categories: "ubiquitous" acts that are numerous and easily accomplished, and "explosive" acts that are more dramatic but more expensive and difficult to implement. As you probably noticed in the list above, some acts will cost little to no money to perform, and others will require a significant investment. All will consistently reinforce each newspaper's role as *its* community's most involved and caring media resource. It's this combination of ubiquitous acts and explosive acts that will make the company's *uncommon offering* well known to its *core customer*.

I'm happy to report that the participants headed for home confident that they now knew how to celebrate their newspaper's Inside Advantage.

CHAPTER 11

Ubiquitous and Explosive Acts

I f you're hungry for additional examples of **OWN IT!**, you're reading the right chapter. My purpose is to offer examples from many kinds of businesses that will inform and inspire your own *imaginative acts*. To maintain focus on the acts and the ideas behind them, I won't describe—as I did for the community newspaper company earlier in the book—the processes that created the strategic framework or the *imaginative acts* but rather will focus on examples of the acts themselves.

Let's take a moment to make the important distinction between the kinds of acts that are available to you and your business. I've already mentioned that some of them cost nothing or very little to perform while others require a significant investment of time as well as human and financial resources to implement. All, of course, must be tightly linked with your company's strategic framework and all must celebrate your Inside Advantage.

Ubiquitous acts can be aimed at every customer touch point—they constitute dozens and dozens of small, usually inexpensive, easy-to-perform actions that work together to create a cumulative impact. The acts must be executed with great frequency, consistency, and uniformity.

Explosive acts, on the other hand, are at touch points that are particularly significant to customers—exciting places, events, and times where customers congregate or on occasions that are personally meaningful to them: life-changing events; large trade shows; annual conventions; big sports venues; community celebrations, national holidays, artificial occasions that your brand or company invents for promotional purposes; and so on. These acts must be powerful and memorable. They must create customer impact. Clearly, they must be done infrequently because they take time, money, and effort to execute. Obviously, they must be flawless in execution, celebratory in their nature, and valuable in terms of offering your firm a good return on its investment.

You can achieve a considerable impact by reinforcing your *uncommon offering* through ubiquitous actions that can be as small as a specific phone greeting used throughout the organization, or a consistent, brief message on all e-mail communications.

One of my clients, a golf products retailer, created ideas that would make it well known for helping golfing enthusiasts achieve their goals through simple acts such as: greeting customers with "Hello, how can I help you achieve your golfing goals?"; creating a training manual for all employees that describes the customer experience the firm is to provide and that insists that this uniform way of thinking and acting become a part of the employees' DNA; and sending a periodic e-mail newsletter that provides "Tips for Our Golfing Enthusiasts" and that features special offers on merchandise.

The golfing firm's explosive acts are big, very innovative, and well designed to have a strong effect on its *core customer*. The company will brand and promote an annual awards ceremony for the area's most respected female and male golfing enthusiasts. This undertaking will link the brand with golfers who have a true passion for the game. To provide extra services for the firm's most loyal and valuable customers, it will establish a "golf concierge" who can arrange tee times and golfing vacations. To encourage potential customers to visit the company's Web site, the firm will provide updated online scoreboards and news about the top golf matches in the area. To assure that it "owns" golf in the community, it will sponsor TV and radio broadcasts of important local or regional golf competitions.

Here's an explosive act from a very different industry. For three years running, Moët & Chandon, the giant champagne producer, has created a highly publicized *imaginative act* for its Rosé Impérial Champagne brand at New York Fashion Week. The company sets up a "Moët Rosé Lounge" in one of the giant white tents in Bryant Park that houses the world-renowned fashion show. Stars of the fashion world and show business stop by to sample the company's offering. It's an expensive endeavor, but it delivers meaningful benefits: it allows the product to be sampled; connects Moët & Chandon with opinion makers; and dramatizes the brand's trendy and celebratory personality. These *imaginative acts* link directly with and dramatize what I believe is the brand's *uncommon offering*: an affordable, accessible nonvintage rosé champagne from a famous, elite French brand. The acts celebrate and unlock the brand's Inside Advantage. Who but Moët could own this particular offering? Franklin D. Isacson, the drink's brand manager, underscored the value of the company's investment and created even more "buzz" with his quote in the *Wall Street Journal*: "Paris Hilton's publicist called me to make sure she could get a VIP pass."

The Cost of Owning It

If you work in a large company like Apple, with ample marketing budgets, most likely you can obtain the funding you require to develop and execute explosive *imaginative acts*. As you've seen in our examples from Moët & Chandon, Neiman Marcus, Tavist, and Apple, the rewards for *imaginative acts* far outweigh the costs.

If you are working with top-echelon management that is accustomed to relying only on conventional communications techniques, you will want to explain the unique benefits of this untraditional initiative and describe how this approach will efficiently enable your brand to own its Inside Advantage.

But what if you don't have the budget to invest in these ideas? You can still become well known to your *core customer* for little or no money. If you doubt this can be done, think about what a small blue box has done for Tiffany & Co. Tiffany's famous robin's-egg-blue box doesn't cost more than any other color box, but now throughout the world that color stands for elegance and quality.

> **BLOOM ON GROWTH**
>
> The rewards for *imaginative acts* far outweigh the costs.

The Internet offers incredible no-cost or low-cost opportunities to target customers, measure responses, engage in dialogue with customers, capitalize on strategic alliances, and, most important, invite potential customers to obtain more information about a product or service via a Web site, e-mail newsletters, e-mail invitations, and more.

My sports and entertainment marketing agency client, STRATEGIC, recently launched a dynamic site—an explosive act for a small company—that demonstrates that it owns its *uncommon offering*. Says its Web site: "We take brands places they've never been."

The site gives life and color to events STRATEGIC has created, such as the U.S. Pond Hockey Championships in Eagle River, Wisconsin, for its Labatt Blue client; valuable sponsorships it has secured, such as the New York Mets Pre-Game Show; and the

Radio City Music Hall's Annual Christmas Spectacular for its North Fork Bank client. Go on www.strategicagency.com to see for yourself how this sports and entertainment marketing specialist has created ideas to take its clients' brands "places they've never been" like the Super Bowl, the Masters Golf Tournament, the World Series, the Sundance Film Festival, down to and including even local bowling alleys. My client also used low- or no-cost ubiquitous acts such as applying its customer promise to its telephone greeting, letterhead, invoices, business cards, and e-mail identity. Next year it's planning a new explosive act: an event at a place its clients and prospects have never been and food and beverages they have never experienced. The company is looking for a venue that will celebrate the Inside Advantage that STRATEGIC offers its clients: taking brands places they've never been.

Internet aside, many of the smaller organizations I have worked with have been able to create explosive *imaginative acts* within their budget. The start-up fitness center mentioned earlier in the book, for example, is planning a quarterly fitness and wellness progress celebration at its facility to stimulate dialogue between clients, potential clients, and trainers. They will serve healthy beverages and snacks and ask customers to bring an interested friend along to join in the action. Attendees can enter a drawing to win workout gear by completing an entry card that supplies the fitness center with the most valuable information of all, a friend's e-mail address.

BLOOM ON GROWTH

> Tiffany's famous robin's-egg-blue box doesn't cost any more than any other color box, but now throughout the world that color stands for elegance and quality.

As you have seen, **OWN IT!** stresses the need to show your *core customer*—as opposed to everyone—that you "own" your *uncommon offering*. Focusing only on the *core customer* makes

OWN IT! cost effective for small local businesses as well as for giant international businesses more accustomed to paying for exposure via mass media.

Whether you do it cheaply or expensively, through ubiquitous acts or explosive ones, *imaginative acts* will celebrate your Inside Advantage. It's in this way that your business' difference begins to manifest itself and you start to gather new customers, repeat customers, and accelerate the growth of your firm.

It's time now to turn to your own company. In the next chapter, I will show you how to generate your own exciting, growth-spurring *imaginative acts*.

CHAPTER 12

Become Well Known for Your Advantage

Just as Victoria's Secret stands for sexy, Wal-Mart stands for everyday low prices, and iPod for cool, your business, through your *imaginative acts*, will stand for the *uncommon offering* you've defined in the Growth Discovery Process. This is how you will fully leverage your business' Inside Advantage.

Through these acts, you will become well known to your *core customer* for your *uncommon offering* and you will unlock your Inside Advantage. This is the exhilarating part of the process, where you are able to draw on your imagination to invent a series of ubiquitous and explosive ideas to **OWN IT!**

I've said this before, but I believe it's important to repeat it: we are not brainstorming in a vacuum—every one of your ideas for *imaginative acts* must fit in the strategic framework that has been built for your business. Please keep this notion firmly in mind as you proceed.

Here is one fascinating *imaginative act* that a company tried in the recent past. We can all take inspiration from it.

> **BLOOM ON GROWTH**
>
> Every one of your ideas for *imaginative acts* must fit in the strategic framework that has been built for your business.

Bubbles Revisited

Perrier has a slew of current *imaginative acts* to win an entire new generation of chic customers here in the United States.

If you're part of this special *core target customer* segment, you may already be participating in Perrier's "Bubbling Under" experience. If not, you can have a virtual experience by going to www.usa.perrier.com where you'll immediately hear the effervescent sound of Perrier's big bubbles. As you navigate the site, you can't help but notice how the brand continues to celebrate its *uncommon offering* with the distinctive sound effects and the eye-catching graphics of green bubbles, colorful stylized people having fun, snapshots of cool celebrities, and trendy events where people are enjoying Perrier.

Perrier's numerous *imaginative acts* are being experienced by the cool crowd at venues where they frequently congregate: the U.S. Comedy Arts Festival in Aspen; the Groundlings, Los Angeles's improvisational school and comedy troupe; the Gen Art's Annual Fashion Week in New York; and the FUNKSHION: Fashion Week Miami Beach that features the fusion of fashion and music. Perrier is all over these events, serving up its "Bubbling Under" award to rising artistic stars and, of course, a lot of big bubbles to everyone who attends.

To reconnect with members of the chic crowd who can't get to these events, Perrier has cooked up some innovative drink recipes to enliven events or parties it may be planning. The drink selection includes the Perrier Slice, the Blue Bazooki, and the Perrier Limonata. The brand has also created some fun party ideas for these local celebrations such as "Not Another Beach Party," the "Spa Party," and the "Zipcode Party." Not stopping there, the wannabe in-crowd is invited to check out pop cultures' most outrageous personalities at Club Perrier.

I would certainly give Perrier a "Bubbling Under" Award for its series of *imaginative acts* tied to its *uncommon offering*. Using **OWN IT!** Perrier will grab the bubbles bunch.

The Imaginative Acts Keep On Coming

Once we get the idea of **OWN IT!**, it seems that we just can't get enough examples of *imaginative acts*. Here are a few others, each illustrating a very different way to become *well known* to a *core customer* for an *uncommon offering*.

TNT

With thousands of obscure TV channels to choose from, why should a viewer choose a station that has such a hodgepodge of programming (basketball, cops and robbers, movies, etc.), and an uninspiring brand name (TNT)? Other channels and, indeed, many companies struggle with similar problems. Many conclude that they can't **OWN IT!** because they have no "it"—no *uncommon offering* to own. They're wrong.

TNT has found a tangible and emotional *uncommon offering*—the "drama" that each program in its wide assortment offers the viewer: the drama of the basketball competition, the drama of the lawful versus the lawless, and the drama in the script and acting of its movies. And it has found an authoritative way to become *well known* for "drama" by consistently communicating "TNT—We Know Drama." Sure, this is a slogan—a good one that's rooted in the station's strategic framework and celebrated in the channel's on-air promos, its TV page ads, and its public relations releases to advertisers, agencies, and viewers. The takeaway is this: every business has an Inside Advantage and there are many ways to **OWN IT!**

Toyota

If your business had 388,000 employees, 10 plants, and a $15-billion investment in a foreign country and wanted to be the number one selling brand in that country, how would you do it? Of course you would try to earn a reputation for quality, reliability, and value—all essential tangible customer benefits. But how would you win customers' enduring respect and loyalty as well as earn the hearts and minds of other vitally important audiences such as current and potential employees, labor unions and local, and state and national government officials? You would do it by showcasing your commitment to that country just as Toyota is doing in the United States.

Wisely, Toyota hasn't tried to do it with a slogan or an "image-building" ad campaign in the United States. The company is rapidly becoming *well known* for its "commitment to America" (**WHAT**), not because of its promises or swagger. The company has set a course to **OWN IT!** with its deeds. Toyota is demonstrating that it is a caring local employer and charitable corporate citizen by supporting the artistic, cultural, civic, and local development initiatives in the communities where it has major operations. It is also funding a vast array of national and local cultural, educational, and environmental programs.

By communicating this honest story of caring, commitment, and philanthropy in a low-key way via its Web site, public relations releases, and dignified corporate ads, Toyota can, over time, deserve a reputation as a valued and respected American citizen. This is further evidence that there are a great many ways to **OWN IT!**

Cabela's

With its 19 fish-and-gun destination megastores in the United States, Cabela's has created an enduring and monumentally explosive *imaginative act*. The company celebrates its position as the "World's Foremost Outfitter" with customer discovery and involvement at every turn and at every moment. Has Cabela's become *well known* for its *uncommon offering*? Well, you know that it does **OWN IT!** when you visit any one of its stores that *The Economist* calls a "retail paradise of outdoor life." Cabela's lives its Inside Advantage, as this description drawn from *The Economist* shows: customers see and experience archery ranges, rows and rows of gleaming fishing rods, huge aquariums, gun shops, shooting galleries, and enormous displays of mounted wildlife of all kinds. They also enjoy the outdoor fare of "ostrich, elk, venison and bison" in the stores' canteens. Creating exciting destination stores designed to attract millions of outdoor enthusiasts is still another way to **OWN IT!**

Boeing

Innovation in aircraft design—here's how to **OWN IT!** The giant aircraft manufacturer Boeing has set up a "Dreamliner Gallery" to help potential customers experience and imagine its new airplane, the 787 Dreamliner, and even try out and select options, just as they would in an automobile dealer's showroom. Representatives from airlines all around the world—including Ethiopian Airlines, Japan Airlines, and Northwest Airlines—visit the Everett, Washington, installation where, as the *Wall Street Journal* points out, they can't kick the tires but they can "try out a variety of seats and even conduct bakeoffs to test how well different flight ovens warm up chocolate-chip cookies. . . . Customers can browse the different makes of seats, entertainment equipment and other add-ons."

Do customers relish the experience? Says the *Wall Street Journal*: "During a recent reception at the showroom, airline repre-

sentatives jumped from seat to seat, pushing all the buttons."
Boeing has succeeded in creating another way to **OWN IT!** with an
explosive *imaginative act*.

Follow These Footsteps and You'll Soon OWN IT!

Ubiquitous and explosive *imaginative acts* will enable your company or brand to become synonymous with your *uncommon
offering*—and your *uncommon offering* to become synonymous
with your company or brand. When this happens, you **OWN IT!**
and your Inside Advantage becomes a powerful weapon against
competition.

Here's my step-by-step procedure to help you **OWN IT!** As
you've done before, please carefully review each and every step.
Individually and collectively, these steps will assist you in creating
imaginative acts for your brand, division, franchise, or company.

1. Begin with a thorough review of the **WHO**, **WHAT**, and
HOW statements that you've already developed. Together,
they become the strategic framework for your *imaginative acts*.
Study every word in this framework before you begin generating ideas. Keep the framework right in front of you, or in
front of you and your team, and create ideas to make your
uncommon offering well known to your *core customer*.

2. Imagination is the essential ingredient in this activity. Don't
trash an idea so long as it's consistent with the strategic framework. Many ideas that sound wacky at the beginning may offer
promise. Did a "Fortnight" sound fabulous at first mention?
Did "Breathe Easier America" sound workable at the start? If
the idea is fresh and different and if it's right for your business
(and your business *alone*), you will probably find a way to make
it work. Be relentless in your efforts to innovate, and above all,

stop dead in your tracks if you have the slightest thought of doing what someone else has already done. How can you be well known with an act that someone has already used?

3. Before proceeding, take a close look at the many *imaginative acts*—some ubiquitous and some explosive—that were created in sessions with my consulting clients. See the "Core Customer **WHO**, **WHAT**, **HOW**, and **OWN IT!** Statements" below. Please read through them—but only for inspiration. Your business is different from every other business, and that includes the ones discussed in this book. It will only grow if your *imaginative acts* pertain exclusively to your *uncommon offering*. Nonetheless, you'll benefit from and perhaps be inspired by the many, many acts imagined by these clients. Note that these are *selected imaginative acts*, a small, carefully chosen group from the many thousands that I have had the honor and the fun of coaxing from my clients.

Core Customer WHO, WHAT, HOW, and OWN IT! Statements

A National Chain of Suburban Newspapers

WHO: An active suburban homeowning family that cares about enhancing its quality of life and learning about local products and services that satisfy its needs and wants

WHAT: Timely, valuable news and information that touches the lives of the local community more consistently and comprehensively than any other source

HOW: Earn the community's trust and respect by helping to make it a better place to live

OWN IT!: See this client's *imaginative acts* in "A Bob Bloom Consulting Session—**OWN IT!**—Finding Our Imaginative Acts"

A West Coast Golf Products Retailer

WHO: An affluent, avid golfer who constantly seeks a better golfing experience

WHAT: Expert advice, customized assistance, and a passion for helping our clients improve their game

HOW: Help golfing enthusiasts achieve their individual goals

OWN IT!: Ubiquitous and explosive *imaginative acts*:

• Communicate the firm's commitment to help golfers achieve their goals via Web site, catalog, "achieving goals" mission on letterhead, business cards, literature, counter cards, packaging, shopping bags, merchandise displays, advertising, and so on.

• Greet every customer with "Hello—how can I help you achieve your golfing goals?"

• Sponsor and promote clinics, troubleshooting sessions, demonstrations of new clubs, balls, and so on.

• E-mail customers after every sale to express appreciation and reaffirm passion for the game.

• Send e-newsletters with "Tips for Our Golfing Enthusiasts," new merchandise, special offers, and so on.

• Set up a "golf concierge" to help the firm's most valuable customers arrange tee times and golf vacations.

• Certify that all sales associates must graduate from an "Advanced School of Golfing" that has been created for the firm by a group of well-known golf champions.

• Develop literature, videos, publicity, and TV commercials about the "Advanced School of Golfing."

- Create an annual awards ceremony to honor the year's most respected local female and male golfing enthusiast.

- Sponsor TV and radio broadcasts of important local or regional golf competitions.

- Use the company's Web site to provide updated scores from top area clubs.

A Global Technology Provider

WHO: A global business enterprise that seeks the expert advice of a technology provider that understands its business

WHAT: A trusting partnership that ensures operational efficiency and valuable intelligence from its customers' technology investment

HOW: Earn a more intimate relationship by tailoring our services to our clients' ever-changing needs

OWN IT!: Ubiquitous and explosive *imaginative acts*:

- Define a "partnership process" that expresses how the firm creates an enduring customer relationship.

- Develop a training manual that assures that this process becomes embedded in the DNA of all employees.

- Arrange an annual meeting of top executives with every customer to assure an effective and efficient ongoing partnership.

- Make the company's partnership process the focal point of the Web site and all customer literature.

- Leverage search engine optimization to assure that the Web site ranks high on key industry terms and buzzwords.

- Consistently reinforce the company's commitment to this "partnership process" at every customer touch point.

- Send periodic e-newsletters to customers and potential customers with news of the company's technology advancements and upgrades.

- Create periodic educational webcast seminars that feature the firm's technical experts.

- Arrange speaking engagements for the firm's top executives at industry meetings and obtain feature articles in important trade publications on the firm's "partnership process."

- Create a blockbuster booth at the annual industry that highlights the company's process.

A Renowned Symphony Orchestra

WHO: A frequent patron of classical music concerts who seeks a more passionate musical experience

WHAT: An orchestra that encourages every musician to share in the creation of an intensely memorable concert

HOW: Deliver visceral audience involvement in each concert

OWN IT!: Ubiquitous and explosive *imaginative acts*:

- Redesign the Web site and literature to emphasize the orchestra's message about its high performance standards.

- Create special events for current and potential subscribers and donors where they can gain an understanding of the orchestra's unique approach to the recruitment of musicians, selection of compositions, and ways to rehearse.

- Establish a "Patrons Group" that enables multiyear subscribers and important donors to experience behind-the-scenes orchestra activities.

- Create and publicize a series of community outreach performances for underprivileged youth and senior citizens.

- Send e-program notes that describe the emotional content of upcoming performances to all subscribers.

- Place banner ads that emphasize the emotional content of upcoming performances on community Web sites.

- Record special performances and provide downloads whenever possible.

- Create a "Young Music Lovers" group to generate attendance from a new generation of concertgoers.

- Employ a public relations agency to secure feature stories about the special way the orchestra performs.

An Ultra-High-End Jewelry Store

WHO: An affluent local male or female status seeker who is looking for a fashion statement

WHAT: An incomparable selection of one-of-a-kind jewelry and watches offered in an elegant private setting

HOW: Create a reputation for an exclusive shopping and buying experience

OWN IT!: Ubiquitous and explosive *imaginative acts*:

- Secure the notice, respect, and admiration of affluent citizens by donating an exceptionally beautiful one-of a-kind jewelry item to the annual charity auction for the benefit of an important civic organization.

- Create a series of elegant private customer events that showcase merchandise that has recently arrived.

- Host receptions for famous international jewelry designers.

- Arrange a series of by-invitation-only fashion shows in partnership with upscale clothing boutiques to showcase elegant jewelry displayed on designer garments.

- Send discreet reminders to customers in advance of their spouse's birthday, anniversary, and holiday giving occasions with an invitation for a private shopping experience.

- Follow up every customer visit with a brief handwritten note and fresh flower bouquet.

- Become the press's most authoritative source on valuable jewelry by providing reporters with expert perspectives and insights whenever possible.

- Honor a local man or woman whose civic contributions have significantly benefited the community and reward that person with a valuable gift at the annual black-tie award event.

A Start-Up Fitness Center

WHO: An adult man or woman who wants and can afford an exceptional personal training experience

WHAT: Consistent progress toward complete personal well-being, planned and monitored by expert trainers and nutritionists

HOW: Provide a system of measurement and expert advice that assures progress toward an individual's evolving health and fitness goals

OWN IT!: Ubiquitous and explosive *imaginative acts*:

- Create a brand name—*metrics*—that reflects the fitness center's *uncommon offering* of "Measured Progress Toward Total Well-Being."

- Adopt a graphic identity and apply it at every customer touch point: uniforms for trainers and nutritionists; client contracts; letterhead; business cards; signage in gym, locker rooms, and nutrition center; invoices; client progress reports; branded work-out merchandise for purchase, and so on.

- Design a Web site that demonstrates the concept of measured progress.

- Send text messages to clients with nutritional advice, especially around mealtimes.

- Send e-mails congratulating clients on their progress.

- Develop a periodic e-mail newsletter featuring real-life (anonymous) client experiences, informative columns by trainers and nutritionists, and news about new gym equipment and workouts.

- Create a video for prospecting that depicts the firm's systematic measurement process, facility, and equipment.

- Create a quarterly "progress celebration" at the center to stimulate dialogue among clients, potential clients, and trainers. Serve healthy beverages and snacks. Offer a drawing for workout gear that captures e-mail addresses of clients' friends.

- Create a booklet that outlines generous incentives for referral of new customers.

A Prominent Wealth Management Firm

WHO: A prospective client with assets of $15+ million to invest plus an intense desire for special services and attention

WHAT: An expert financial advisor who delivers an unrivaled portfolio of customized services and exceptional investment results

HOW: Demonstrate the value of our services to clients and those that influence them to earn their loyalty and advocacy with prospective clients

OWN IT!: Ubiquitous and explosive *imaginative acts*:

• Develop a brochure that describes the firm's history, portfolio of customized services for high-net-worth individuals and families, and notable investment performance.

• Create individual booklets on the firm's expertise in specialized assets: airplanes, ranches, boats, oilfields, real estate, and so on.

• Invite clients to series of exclusive events to demonstrate performance and appreciation and ask them to bring family members, legal and accounting resources, and friends interested in hearing a guest panel of distinguished industry and public officials discuss the nation's economy.

• Familiarize "influencers" of current and potential clients (attorneys, tax counselors, and management specialists) with the company's unique portfolio of special services.

• Redesign the Web site to focus on the customized portfolio of services, placing somewhat less emphasis on the investment performance.

• Leverage search engine optimization to assure that the Web site ranks high on keywords associated with management of airplanes, ranches, boats, oilfields, real estate, and so on.

An Upscale Chain of Tanning Salons

WHO: An image-conscious single woman who wants to look and feel better with little investment in time or money

WHAT: A tanning experience that exceeds customer expectations regarding amenities, privacy, and price

HOW: Invite tanners to experience our unique tanning salon without cost or obligation

OWN IT!: Ubiquitous and explosive *imaginative acts*:

- Because customer conversion is exceptionally high after the free trial, focus the firm's resources on generating trials, providing a customer experience that exceeds expectations and immediately converts to a sale.

- Redesign the Web site to invite a free trial via enticing special offers.

- Utilize telephone greeting and window signs to attract trial.

- Train personnel and offer incentives to convert inquiry to trial and trial to contract.

- Offer special incentives to current customers to refer friends and workmates to try the firm's tanning experience.

- Create a special Web site where customers can upload their pictures, experiment with different skin tone solutions, and customize their tans.

- Use banner ads on Web sites that correlate with tanning (travel, parties, proms, graduation, etc.).

- Establish periodic e-communication with customers that seeks feedback and offers generous incentives for referrals.

- Establish a 24-hour hotline so that customers can report any experience that is inconsistent with their expectations.

- Create a periodic online newsletter featuring a "Tanning Trends" column, a "My Tan, My Life" column written by a satisfied (anonymous) customer, new tanning product introductions, special seasonal promotions, generous incentives for referrals, and so on.

A Sports and Entertainment Marketing Agency

WHO: A powerful marketer with a big ad budget that demands results-driven sponsorship programs

WHAT: Transfer the excitement, positive values, and dynamic imagery of sports and entertainment to brands

HOW: Take brands places they have never been and prove that we deliver results

OWN IT!: Ubiquitous and explosive *imaginative acts*:

- Center all external communications on "Taking Brands Places They've Never Been"—give it meaning and credibility.

- Redesign Web site that utilizes this differentiating statement in imaginative ways. Provide online video case studies of clients who have achieved success.

- Create a periodic e-newsletter featuring a "Places Our Brands Are Going" column written by a client, with news of the agency's progress, profiles of staff, and so on.

- Create a unique annual event for clients and prospects at a "place they've never been."

- Arrange speaking engagements at major advertising and marketing conferences to describe the benefits and results of "Taking Brands Places They've Never Been."

- Employ a public relations agency to obtain feature articles in important advertising and marketing publications to reinforce the agency's mission.

- Send a series of innovative mailers to prospects with memorabilia of exciting places the agency has taken brands: tennis sneakers from the U.S. Open, football from Super Bowl, pennant from the Indy 500, and so on.

A Publisher of Insurance Industry Data, News, and Other Information

WHO: A financial professional who provides advice and solutions to clients who want or need to be better informed about insurance

WHAT: The insurance industry's authoritative and comprehensive source of information, data, and analysis

HOW: Make our products and services indispensable to daily decision making

OWN IT!: Ubiquitous and explosive *imaginative acts*:

- Redesign Web site to demonstrate how and why the firm is the authoritative, indispensable source for all insurance-related data, information, and news by showcasing the broad range of publications, newsletters, conferences, and data sources that the firm publishes.

- Establish a uniform way to describe the company's services and products in this differentiating context and utilize this language in all internal and external communications.

- Leverage search engine optimization to assure that the Web site ranks high on subjects vital to financial professionals.

- Employ a respected research organization to conduct an annual objective survey of financial professionals' views of industry trends. Publicize the survey findings on the opening day of the industry's most important convention.

- Employ a public relations agency to establish the firm as the most authoritative source on all matters relating to the insurance industry.

A Not-for-Profit Social Services Organization

WHO: An individual, a family, or a community that is underserved in terms of urgent human needs and lack of resources

WHAT: An organization dedicated to meeting the evolving health, living, and nutritional needs of the underserved in our community

HOW: Conduct and publish a comprehensive survey of our community's changing needs every two years

OWN IT!: Ubiquitous and explosive *imaginative acts*:

- Revise the company's internal and external communications to reflect its commitment to serve the changing needs of the community.

- Study the best practices of organizations that serve the needs of the underserved in other urban areas.

- Solicit the cooperation, advice, and support of health-care providers, support groups, educational institutions, and advocacy groups.

- Familiarize corporations, foundations, trusts, and individuals with the findings of the company's survey on the community's changing needs and aggressively seek their funding of early intervention initiatives.

- Recruit national and local celebrities to endorse, be involved in, and raise funds for the company's new programs.

- Secure involvement of educational institutions and government organizations that study the changing realities of the underserved in urban populations.

- Publish a book that documents the vision, strategies, programs, and accomplishments of the organization.

- Become the most reliable source for facts, information, and programs devoted to the underserved.

---

4. Keep these rules of the road firmly in mind:

- **Make your *uncommon offering* well known to your *core customer*.** Don't waste resources trying to become well known to everyone.

- Create *imaginative acts* to be well known for your *uncommon offering.* Don't create *imaginative acts* just to be well known.

- Enhance your *uncommon offering.* A vibrant, intimate, comprehensive customer experience will help assure the retention of current customers and provide fresh ways to recruit new ones.

> Don't waste resources trying to become
> well known to everyone.

- Create ubiquitous *imaginative acts* that reinforce your *uncommon offering.* These initiatives must be executed with frequency, consistency, and uniformity.

- Invent a few explosive *imaginative acts* to dramatize your *uncommon offering.* These initiatives must be cleverly conceived, flawlessly executed, and unique to your enterprise. Don't undertake more explosive *imaginative acts* than you and your company can afford and you can manage effectively—one or two, but no more than four per year.

The ubiquitous and explosive *imaginative acts* will supplement and complement each other. Working efficiently together in this way, they will enable your firm to become well known to your *core customer* for its *uncommon offering.* That's what **OWN IT!** is all about.

You are ready to create **OWN IT!** for your business. But before we move on, please look through the frequently asked questions that follow on the next page. The list may answer any questions you have about generating ideas for your *imaginative acts.*

The Inside Advantage FAQ—OWN IT!

Q: Can it be very easy to become well known?

A: It isn't easy to become well known for your business difference. **OWN IT!** requires imagination, hard work, and consistency. It will also take a little patience, as your *core customer* will need some time to become aware of your message, believe it, and be motivated to try your service or product. Given today's skeptical customer, you'll probably get only one chance to deliver your *uncommon offering*. Companies that are well known for consistently meeting or exceeding customer expectations will experience growth; companies that aren't consistently meeting or exceeding customer expectations won't grow and may suffer even worse consequences. Becoming well known for the way you are different from your competitors isn't easy and won't happen overnight, but not being different and well known is likely to end in failure.

Q: What exactly do you mean by *imaginative*?

A: My dictionary lists many meanings of *imaginative*. The one I like most in the context of **OWN IT!** is "showing a command of imagery." I suggest that you look at each act to determine if it exhibits your firm's command of imagery and if it reflects and magnifies your Inside Advantage.

Q: You mention "customer touch points" quite a lot. I think I know what you mean, but please define the term for me.

A: Customer touch points are any time the customer interacts with your business. Any time! That means when she casually walks down the street in front of your building or shop; when he shops your Web site; when she calls, e-mails, or faxes you; when he or she sees an ad or TV commercial or hears a radio commercial or receives a brochure, mailer, or invitation; when the recipient opens a gift purchased at your shop; when there is a transaction with your firm; any time your service or product is being used or consumed; when your company is contacted about a product or service problem; and so on. All touch points are important, but many will determine whether your customer remains loyal to your business or moves on and whether your customer recommends your firm or trashes it. Touch points are all about the customers' interaction with your Inside Advantage and the entire customer experience you deliver.

Q: Should I be worried about using Web sites, e-mails, and public relations, as these ubiquitous acts might also be used by others, including my competitors?

A: There will be similarities in some of the *fundamental* methods or tools you use to become well known, but not in *how you express your imaginative acts* or how you *tie your imaginative acts to your business*. Fundamentals like blocking and tackling in football and order and precision in battle are crucial to the victor, but it is *how the victor executes these fundamentals* that make him the winner on the playing field or the battlefield. Fundamental ubiquitous acts like adding an expression of your *uncommon offering* to your e-mail or calling card will be similar firm to firm, but it's *how* you do it and *how* you tie it to your firm's name that will make you stand out. You will need many ubiquitous acts, some that may be quite fundamental and others that must be quite special. Quantity is essential, but it's your creativity, passion, and consistency that will enable you to **OWN IT!**

Q: How many *imaginative acts* should I create and implement?

A: There is no right or wrong number. So, I'll answer this question in a variety of ways; you should create and implement (a) one or more at every customer touch point; (b) as many as you can afford; (c) as many as you can create and deliver well and effectively; (d) the quantity that will create a series of acts;

and/or (e) the quantity that will make your *uncommon offering* well known to your *core customer* and unlock and own your Inside Advantage.

Q: How do I decide whether an *imaginative act* is ubiquitous or explosive?

A: In the end, whether it is one or the other will become obvious, but the label you put on an *imaginative act* is irrelevant. Start by inventing, not by characterizing an act as one thing or another. Concentrate on making each one fresh and ownable. After you've pushed the envelope on creativity, look at the acts together. All your *imaginative acts* must make your *uncommon offering* well known to your *core customer*. All must be executed consistently and flawlessly. The numerous ubiquitous acts must be frequent and at every customer touch point—the few explosive acts must be blockbusters and at very special customer touch points.

Q: In an earlier FAQ, you say that it is essential to get the person responsible for sales to commit to **HOW**. I'm interested in knowing why this is so important and whether it's relevant to **OWN IT!**

A: It's essential to get your head of sales to agree to **HOW** because he or she is probably the best person in the room to judge whether your *persuasive strategy* will resonate with your customers. Moreover, it's your head of sales who must deliver the supplemental revenue to fuel your growth, so you don't want that person to have any excuses for underperformance—for not selling more of your **WHAT** to your **WHO**. You don't want to hear your sales head saying after the fact, "You know, I was never very excited about the **HOW** we came up with." Rather, you want to him or her to be willing to state, without equivocation, to *every participant* in the room, "This is a *persuasive strategy* that my sales team will get behind full force—it will help us deliver the sales increases we need to grow." With that kind of enthusiastic acceptance in place, you can move on with confidence to the creation of your **OWN IT!** and your *imaginative acts*. When you, your sales head, and every participant in the room enthusiastically agree that you have nailed your **HOW**, your **OWN IT!** can't help but make your *uncommon offering* well known to your *core customer*.

You're Ready to Grow

Growing a business is one of life's most stimulating and fulfilling undertakings. Yet, from personal experience, I know that it's challenging and, at times, a little frightening. However, you have the wind at your back. You know your craft and you've had the intellectual curiosity to learn how to craft a growth strategy and unlock your business's Inside Advantage.

What's required now is determination, perseverance, and, of course, some luck. It's been my experience that if you have the determination and perseverance, you will make your own luck.

Still, I'll wish you good luck, good success—and a hearty, growth-spurring Inside Advantage.

Make Growth Happen–NOW!

F rom the first page of this book to this, its conclusion, I've had but one goal: *simplify the task of growing your business.* I hope that my career experiences and personal perspectives as reflected in these pages have convinced you that sustained profitable growth is achievable as well as essential. Today, no company can survive or thrive without growth.

The urgent and severe challenges that every twenty-first-century business faces have made it impossible for any company, large or small, to survive by standing still. Thus, I urge you to get started on the road to growth without delay.

Wake Up Your Dormant Inside Advantage

If you feel your brand or firm is not realizing its full potential, read these few final pages. Kick-start the growth of your business by organizing a one-day session focused on the Growth Discovery Process — just like the ones I have been describing throughout the book. You'll find complete instructions here for running one, and even a suggested agenda.

 Sustained profitable growth is achievable as well as essential.

The most robust ideas and the most meaningful results from your Growth Discovery Process session will occur if you assemble a group of 5 to 10 people to participate over a full day. You should invite only those whom you trust and respect, perhaps senior executives from your firm or successful business leaders and advisors from the outside such as a banker, attorney, professor, or accountant. You want people with core competencies that supplement and complement yours — energetic people who will add objectivity, perspective, and imagination — aggressive people with some strategic experience and the guts to speak their minds.

You want a comfortable room, preferably offsite where privacy and quiet can be assured. You'll need three sturdy easels with large flip charts, marking pens in various colors, and masking tape to fix the charts to the walls.

The following procedures will help you proceed efficiently:

1. The time set aside for the session, preferably a full day, must be uninterrupted. To assure that everyone is prepared to participate from minute one, I suggest that you give each participant a copy of this book well in advance of the session and insist that he or she read it before everyone gets together.

2. You can facilitate the session or appoint someone who will be objective and capable of moving the session forward effectively. Everyone in the room must be empowered to participate as equals, and to emphasize this, I recommend that you appoint

each participant "chief strategy officer" for the day. The pace must be vigorous; a spirit of candor and optimism must prevail.

3. In the course of the day, develop statements for the first three components in the Growth Discovery Process that add up to no more than 50 or so vivid, descriptive, and accurate words. All three components must work together in total harmony.

4. The group must achieve total consensus on every word. Keep editing and improving the statements. If you get stuck, put your work aside and move on, as you may find ways to enhance them as you proceed. The strategic framework that's created must be ambitious but achievable. You want to inspire your business to grow profitably, not transform it.

5. Here's an agenda that has worked well in my own consulting and that you may want to consider:

8:00–8:30

☐ Assemble for morning coffee.

☐ If attendees do not know one another, spend a few minutes getting acquainted.

8:30–9:00

☐ Outline a few rules for the session—one mid-morning and one mid-afternoon break; lunch brought in; no phones or BlackBerry devices allowed inside.

☐ Describe the spirit of meeting—no idea is bad; momentum must be maintained; participation from all is essential; total consensus is vital. Explain that brevity is critical and that words and phrases that sound like advertising, jargon, or bravado be avoided. The group must seek words that are meaningful, fresh, and essential to comprehension.

☐ Discuss the objective—creating a strategic framework for growth and a series of *imaginative acts* to highlight and dramatize the firm's Inside Advantage.

☐ Prepare handouts of the Growth Discovery Process and briefly review its sequence.

9:00–10:30

☐ Define **WHO:** the *core customer* most likely to buy your product or service in the quantity required for optimal profit.

10:30–10:45

☐ Break.

10:45–12:15

☐ Define **WHAT:** the *uncommon offering* that your business will own and leverage.

12:15–1:00

☐ Lunch in with a relaxing and liberating atmosphere. Talk about anything but the session.

1:00–2:30

☐ Define **HOW:** the *persuasive strategy* that will convince your *core customer* to buy your *uncommon offering* versus all competitive offerings.

2:30–2:45

☐ Break.

2:45–5:00

☐ **OWN IT!:** the series of *imaginative acts* that will celebrate your *uncommon offering* and make it well known to your *core customer.* All *imaginative acts* must be tightly linked to your strategic framework.

5:00–5:30

☐ Gain enthusiastic agreement to the Growth Discovery Process that's been created.

☐ Commit participants to immediately establish a definitive plan of action to exploit the firm's Inside Advantage using the results of the session. I suggest that you share it via e-mail with all participants for their perspectives.

☐ Thanks to all and celebration.

The session requires a great deal of discipline and organization; however, it will prove to be one of the most fulfilling and thrilling moments in your career as it has been in mine. In one day you will create the strategic framework and *imaginative acts* to grow your business.

Exploit Your Inside Advantage

On the first working day after the session, establish a definitive plan of action to assure the flawless implementation of *imaginative acts* and the consistent delivery of the company's Inside Advantage to all customers. Involve anyone in your organization who is required to implement the plan. If some or all were not participants in the session, take them through the strategic framework and *imaginative acts* that were created. Inspire them to share your optimism and commitment and immediately involve them in the preparation of the plan. If you are a company of one, it's your job to get it done, although you might want to recruit some help from one or two of the work session participants, particularly those that can provide planning experience and objectivity.

Your plan must specify actions for each and every *imaginative act*, timetables, responsibilities, and realistic budgets. If you want to grow, you have to have the determination to execute your plan quickly and flawlessly. You may recall that in one of my client sessions I offered these guidelines for selecting among and organizing the many acts: consistency with the *persuasive strategy*, bang for the buck, ease and speed of execution, and anticipated result.

It is important to create a "scorecard" for each *imaginative act* that you plan to implement. You're looking for a very simple and objective way to evaluate the cost, ease of implementation, anticipated benefit from each act—a way that fits into your current analytical processes for sales, budgeting, and other financial issues. Keep monitoring every individual act after implementation to assure that it's contributing to results and by all means keep adding new *imaginative acts* to maintain impact.

Remember that all the acts do not have to be implemented simultaneously. But do consider performing them in relatively close proximity over time to assure they combine to form a series of acts. That way you will increase awareness among your potential customers and provide a more powerful dramatic statement. You want numerous easy, low-cost ubiquitous acts and just a few of the more expensive, difficult-to-perform explosive acts.

The strategic framework and program for *imaginative acts* that you create should be regarded as a confidential internal strategic blueprint for your growth. It should not be shared with customers, but it must be shared with your entire staff or organization just prior to implementation together with the implementation plan. I suggest that you hold a staff meeting to explain how it was created, why it will help your firm grow, and why growth will directly benefit them as a group and as individuals.

Emphasize that you will personally "live" the ideas and expressions represented in the plan and that it will guide everything your firm does from this point forward. And then do what you say you're going to do—it cannot be another "New Year's resolution" to be quickly forgotten. The goal of this plan is to fully exploit your Inside Advantage and jump-start your growth.

As the mix of ubiquitous and explosive acts rolls out, your customers and potential customers will feel the impact, and you will begin to feel a difference in your business. Once you begin to see the growth, you can accelerate it by prudently investing in fresh, new *imaginative acts* that will highlight and dramatize your Inside Advantage.

Grow with Your Inside Advantage — NOW!

It is my belief that the greatest enemy to business survival is inaction. The competitors in your industry, your neighborhood, and your world are hungry for new customers. Their appetite will intensify as globalization and technology create scale and cutting-edge benefits for everyone, especially for those with money, muscle, and staying power.

BLOOM ON GROWTH You must be the driving force behind your growth strategy–don't delegate.

But, now *you* have an Inside Advantage. Find it and make it well known to customers and potential customers. Use it to create the magic moment we talked about earlier—the moment when potential customers start buying your products and services and not your competitors'.

If your company, brand, or division needs growth, you must be the driving force behind your growth strategy—don't delegate.

Pushing the task downstairs or upstairs won't work because no one knows your business like you do. And, postponing your growth initiative is likely to have disastrous consequences for your business, your career, and potentially, your life. So, as soon as you close this book, start using the Growth Discovery Process to generate the profitable growth your business urgently needs. With your relentless determination and Inside Advantage, you will over-come all obstacles.

Thanks for reading my book, and good luck in unlocking your Inside Advantage!

NOTES

Introduction: Your Inside Advantage Is the Key to Growth

4   *My mission was defined by the brilliant*: Maurice Levy, "Maurice Levy: How to be a Great Leader," Interview with Todd Benjamin, *CNN.com*, June 24, 2005.

Part 1: CORE CUSTOMERS: WHO Are They?

Chapter 1: The Most Important Word in Business

14   *Procter & Gamble (P&G), one of the largest, most profitable consumer products companies*: Deborah Ball, "Women in Italy Like to Clean but Shun the Quick and Easy," *Wall Street Journal*, April 25, 2006, p. A1.

20   *Let's look at how a business in China*: R. Scott Macintosh, "In China, a Golf Community on a Supergrand Scale," *International Herald Tribune*, September 30, 2005, p. 22.

24   *A close look at the dairy products industry in Asia*: Adam Thompson and Shai Oster, "NBA in China Gets Milk to Sell Hoops," *Wall Street Journal*, January 22, 2007, p. B1.

Chapter 2: All Customers Are Not Created Equal

31   *Gap clothing chain's recent makeover didn't work*: Louise Lee, "Paul Pressler's Fall from the Gap," *BusinessWeek*, February 26, 2007.

31   *As industry executive Paul R. Charron said about Gap's failed effort*: Michael Barbaro and Hillary Chura, "The Gap Is in Need of a Niche," *New York Times*, January 27, 2007, p. C1.

31   *Gap has a new president now*: Amy Merrick, "Gap Chief Offers Harsh Diagnosis," *Wall Street Journal*, March 2, 2007, p. B4.

33   *Match.com recently found a way*: Sara Silver, "How Match.com Found Love Among Boomers," *Wall Street Journal*, January 27, 2007, p. 1.

Chapter 3: Zero In on Your Core Customer

41   *Recently, the great advertising entrepreneur:* Maurice
Saatchi, "The Strange Death of Modern Advertising,"
Financial Times, June 22, 2006, p. 17.

Part 2: UNCOMMON OFFERINGS—WHAT
Can You Offer Them?

Chapter 4: What Business Are You *Really* In?

68   *Here's the good news about Alfa:* Adrian Michaels and John
Reed, "Sales drive plan for Alfa and Lancia," *Financial Times,*
November 10, 2006, p. 24.

72   *AES Engineering, based in the United Kingdom, produces
commonplace engineering seals:* Peter Marsh, "The Masters
of Good Service Manufacturing Strategy," *Financial Times,*
June 30, 2006, p. 9.

73   *Right now India is facing this huge challenge:* Jonathan
Birchall and Jo Johnson, "Mom and Pop Stores Braced for
Wal-Mart," *Financial Times,* November 28, 2006, p. 23.

77   *The* Wall Street Journal *put it this way:* Christopher Lawton
and Joan S. Lublin, "Dell's Founder Returns as CEO," *Wall
Street Journal,* February 1, 2007, p. A1.

Chapter 5: Where Tangible Meets Emotional

88   *Kevin and Jackie Freiberg, the authors of* Nuts!: Kevin L.
Freiberg and Jacquelyn A. Freiberg, *Nuts! Southwest Airlines'
Crazy Recipe for Business and Personal Success,* reprint edi-
tion, (New York: Broadway Books, 1998), p. 38.

90   *In 1986, when it was introduced to the U.S. domestic market:*
Joseph B. White, "Ford Banks on Taurus Revival," *Wall Street
Journal,* February 14, 2007, p. D10.

90   *An automotive writer recently described the Taurus as:* Nick
Bunkley, "Ford Will Resurrect the Taurus Brand," *New York
Times,* February 7, 2007, p. C4.

91   *As the* Wall Street Journal *sees it, the company's declining fortunes:* William M. Bulkeley and Angela Pruitt, "Kodak Sees

More Job Cuts, Higher Restructuring Costs," *Wall Street Journal*, February 9, 2007, p. B4.

Part 3: PERSUASIVE STRATEGIES—HOW Do You Convince Them?

Chapter 7: A Platform Built for One

117   *SKF, a Swedish company:* Peter, Marsh, "Back on a roll in the business of bearings," *Financial Times*, February 7, 2007.

Chapter 8: Stand Out by Standing Alone

123   *The* Wall Street Journal *has flatteringly described Apple's products:* Lee Gomes, "Apple's 30 Years of Selling Cool Stuff With Uncool Message," *Wall Street Journal*, April 5, 2006.

124   *Apple reported an 88 percent increase in profits:* Laurie J. Flynn, "Apple Zooms Past Rivals, with 88% Profit Growth," *New York Times*, April 26, 2007, p. C3.

124   *The introduction of Apple's new mobile telephone:* Kevin Allison, "Apple Faithful Smitten to the Core with iPhone," *Financial Times*, January 10, 2007, p. 25.

125   *As a writer in* The Economist *put it:* "Searching for the Invisible Man. Economics Rediscovers the Entrepreneur," *The Economist*, March 11, 2006, pp. 68–69.

130   *How would you like to be the company:* Ian Bickerton, "TomTom's Road Less Travelled," *Financial Times*, February 22, 2007, p. 8.

130   *Yet Faber-Castell, the venerable pencil manufacturer:* "Face Value. At the Sharp End," *The Economist*, March 3, 2007, p. 73.

Chapter 9: Create a Compelling Persuasive Strategy

133   *The* Wall Street Journal *reported that restructuring costs:* William M. Bulkeley and Angela Pruitt, "Kodak Sees More Job Cuts, Higher Restructuring Costs," *Wall Street Journal*, February 9, 2007, p. B4.

133   *And the* Financial Times *described a much smaller:* Jonathan
       Moules, "Why Some Start-Ups Finish Badly," *Financial
       Times*, November 16, 2005, p. 9.

Part 4: IMAGINATIVE ACTS—OWN IT!

Chapter 10: Never Stop Celebrating Your Advantage

155   *In a speech to British, French, and Italian manufacturing
       groups:* Stanley Marcus, *Minding the Store* (Boston: Little,
       Brown and Company, 1974), p. 205.

156   *To gain the involvement of the entire Dallas community:*
       Stanley Marcus, *Minding the Store* (Boston: Little, Brown
       and Company, 1974), p. 207.

156   *Stanley proudly described the ribbon cutting at the store in
       this way:* Stanley Marcus, *Minding the Store* (Boston: Little,
       Brown and Company, 1974), p. 210.

157   *Here's the way Stanley expressed the results of the French
       Fortnight:* Stanley Marcus, *Minding the Store* (Boston: Little,
       Brown and Company, 1974), p. 210.

Chapter 11: Ubiquitous and Explosive Acts

175   *For three years running, Moët & Chandon, the giant cham-
       pagne producer:* Sarah Nassauer, "How Moët & Chandon
       Made Rosé Champagne Fashionable," *Wall Street Journal*,
       February 15, 2007, p. B1.

Chapter 12: Become Well Known for Your Advantage

183   *Well, you know that it does OWN IT!:* "Hunting, Shooting
       and . . . Shopping," *The Economist*, December 16, 2007, p. 65.

183   *The giant aircraft manufacturer Boeing has set up a
       "Dreamliner Gallery":* J. Lynn Lunsford, "High Design:
       Boeing Lets Airlines Browse," *Wall Street Journal*, February
       14, 2007, p. B1.

Index

Advertising (*See specific topics*)
AES Engineering, 72
Alfa Romeo, 68–69
Apple, 123–125
Applebee's, 65
Art Site, 133
Attraction, of customer to product, 29–30, 56, 60–61

Barbara K, 74
Bharti Enterprises, India, 73
Bloom, Sam R., 3
Bloom Agency, 3–10, 88
　(*See also specific companies*)
BMW, 21–22, 30–31, 92, 116
Boeing, 183–184
Bourgery, Marc, 8, 152–153
Brand transformation, 121–122
Braniff, 89
"Breathe Easier America Day" campaign, 154
Budget for imaginative acts (OWN IT!), 162–163, 176–177, 207–208
BusinessWeek, 31

Cabela's, 183
Celebrating advantage (*See* Imaginative acts [OWN IT!])
Charrin, Paul R., 31
Chili's, 65
China
　dairy products, 24

golf courses, 20–21
Chu, Ken and David, 20–21
Commodity products
　persuasive strategies (HOW), 117–118
　vs. uncommon offerings (WHAT), 69–75, 79–81
Communication of message
　consistent, and growth, 20–23
　nontraditional methods, 160–163
　(*See also* Imaginative acts [OWN IT!])
Competition, 111–112, 123–132
　(*See also* Persuasive strategies [HOW])
Consulting examples
　HOW statements, 135–138
　OWN IT! statements, 164–172
　WHAT statements, 96–99
　WHO statements, 43–49
Core customers (WHO), 13–56
　consistent message and growth, 20–23
　evolution, 23–26
　explosive acts, 177–178
　focus on, 14
　genuine understanding vs. demographic knowledge, 14–17
　Growth Discovery Process, 18–23
　help and inspiration for, 99, 106

Core customers (WHO)
    (*continued*)
    mental picture of, 17–18
    most valuable, 29–31
    persuasive strategies (HOW),
        112–116
    tangible benefits, 87
    targeting, 23–40
    ubiquitous acts, 174–175,
        177–178
    and uncommon offerings
        (WHAT), 21, 25
    WHO statements, 41–56
    (*See also* Persuasive strategies
        [HOW])
Core target audience (*See*
    Targeting core customers)
Cost for imaginative acts (OWN
    IT!), 162–163, 176–177,
    207–208
Creation overview
    HOW statements, 133–135
    OWN IT! statements, 179–180
    WHAT statements, 95–96
    WHO statements, 20–23, 41–44
Current vs. potential customers,
    WHO statements, 47, 55
Curves, 75
"Customer," as most important
    word, 14
    (*See also* Core customers
        [WHO])
Customer touch points (*See* Touch
    points)

Dairy products, China, 24
De Beers, 129

Dell, 77–78
Dell, Michael, 78
Demographics
    customer similarity, 32–34
    vs. genuine understanding of
        core customers, 14–17
Diamonds, 128–129
Dotson, Robert, 8, 121–122

Eastman Kodak, 91, 133
The Economist, 125, 130–131, 183
Emotional benefits
    imaginative acts (OWN IT!),
        181
    persuasive strategies (HOW),
        145, 158
    uncommon offerings (WHAT),
        60–61, 63, 83–93, 101, 106
Endorsements, 36–37
Evolution of customer, targeting,
    23–26
Exercise for women, 75
Experience offerings, 60–62
Explosive acts, 173–178
    core customers, 177–178
    defined, 165, 174, 200
    Internet, 176–177
    step-by-step development,
        184–185

Faber-Castell, 130–131
Faber-Castell, Anton Wolfgang von,
    130–131
FAQs
    HOW statements, 144–145
    OWN IT! statements, 197–201
    WHAT statements, 104–107

WHO statements, 54–56

FDA (U.S. Food and Drug Administration), 151–152

FedEx, 92

FedEx Kinko's, 92

Fiat, 68–69

Financial Times
  persuasive strategies (HOW), 117–118, 124–125, 130
  uncommon offerings (WHAT), 68, 72–73

Flawed offerings, 67–69

Ford Motor Company, 22–23, 90–91

Fortnights, Neiman Marcus, 118–120, 155–157

France, Perrier, 6, 70–71, 180–181

Freiberg, Kevin and Jackie, 88

Gap, 31

Gender
  exercise for women, 75
  targeting core customers, 34–35
  tools for women, 74

Genuine understanding vs. demographic knowledge of core customers, 14–17

Globalization, as challenge, 10

Goals
  HOW statements, 144–145
  OWN IT! statements, 197–198
  WHAT statements, 106
  WHO statements, 54–55

Goddijn, Harold, 130

Golf courses, China, 20–21

Golf Research Group, 20

Google, 41–42, 76

Growth, Inside Advantage as key to, 1–10
  (*See also specific topics*)

Growth Discovery Process
  core customers (WHO), 13–56
  imaginative acts (OWN IT!), 148–201
  one-day group session, 203–207
  overview, 2, 8–10
  persuasive strategies (HOW), 111–145
  summary chart, 7
  uncommon offerings (WHAT), 59–107

Hansen, Marka, 31

Heavin, Gary and Diane, 75

Honesty, persuasive strategies (HOW), 114, 128–129

HOW statements, 133–145
  consulting example, 135–138
  creation overview, 133–135
  emotional connection, 145
  FAQs, 144–145
  goals of, 144–145
  length of, 143
  sample statements, 140–143
  step-by-step development, 138–140
  (*See also* Persuasive strategies [HOW])

H&R Block, 78

Hug Your Customers (Mitchell), 160

Imaginative, defined, 198

Imaginative acts (OWN IT!), 148–201
  celebrating advantage, 149–172

Imaginative acts (OWN IT!)
(*continued*)
consulting examples, 164–172
cost, 162–163, 176–177,
207–208
customer touch points, 198–199
examples, 163–164
explosive acts, 173–178
Growth Discovery Process
chart, 7
inventing, 151–160
magical moments, 150–151
nontraditional communication
methods, 160–163
number of, 199
OWN IT! statements, 179–201
persuasive strategies (HOW),
118–120
plan of action, 207–209
ubiquitous acts, 173–178
India, giant retail expansion into, 73
Inside Advantage
drive for growth, 209–210
origins, 3–6, 88
overview, 1–10
as strategic asset, 1–2
(*See also* Growth Discovery
Process)
Inspiration, of customers, 106
International Herald Tribune, 20
Internet
as challenge, 10
explosive acts, 176–177
Intimate images of core customers
(WHO), 17–18
Inventing imaginative acts (OWN
IT!), 151–160

iPods and iPhones, 123–125, 158
Irrelevance, addressing, 90–92
Isacson, Franklin D., 175
Italy
Alfa Romeo and Fiat, 68–69
cleaning products, 14–15

Jobs, Steve, 124–125, 157–159
Johnstone, Tom, 117–118
Juicy Juice
core customers (WHO), 24–25,
29
imaginative acts (OWN IT!),
163–164
persuasive strategies (HOW),
127
uncommon offerings (WHAT),
79–81

Kelleher, Herb, 88
King, Rollin, 88
Kinko's, 92
Kodak, 91, 133

Length (number of words)
HOW statements, 143
WHAT statements, 104–105
WHO statements, 55
Levy, Maurice, 4
L'Oréal, 60–61, 92, 159
Loyalty of customers, 2, 29–31
LUV (Southwest Airlines), 87–89

Macintosh computer, 124, 157–158
MacMahon, Paul, 25
Magical moments in imaginative
acts (OWN IT!), 150–151

Marcus, Stanley, 8, 16–17, 118–120, 155–157

Marketing (*See specific topics*)

Marriott, J.W. (Bill), Jr., 5

Marriott, J.W., Sr., 5

Marriott Corporation, 5

Match.com, 33–34

McCann, Jim, 132

Mengniu Milk, 24

Mental picture of core customers (WHO), 17–18

Microsoft, 124

Mission Hills development, China, 20–21

Mission vs. WHAT statements, 101

Mitchell, Jack, 34, 159–160

Moët & Chandon, 175

Mulally, Alan, 90

Munster, Eugene A., 124

Muse, Lamar, 88

Neiman Marcus, 16–17, 118–120, 155–157

Nestlé (*See* Juicy Juice)

Nestlé Waters SA, 71–72

New core customers (*See* Targeting core customers)

Novartis (Sandoz), 6, 114–116, 151–155

Nuts! (Freiberg), 88

Obsolete offerings, 90–92

1-800-FLOWERS, 131–132

OTC (over-the-counter) medication conversion, 151–155

Over-the-counter (OTC) medication conversion, 151–155

OWN IT! statements, 179–201

consulting examples, 164–172

creation overview, 179–180

examples, 180–184

FAQs, 197–201

goal of, 197–198

sample statements, 185–197

step-by-step development, 184–185

(*See also* Imaginative acts [OWN IT!])

Perrier, 6, 70–71, 180–181

Persuasive strategies (HOW), 111–145

brand transformation, 121–122

for challenging customers, 114–116

vs. commoditization, 117–118

competition awareness, 111–112

and core customers (WHO), 112–114

elements of, 125–127

examples, 123–125, 130–132

focused, 129

Growth Discovery Process chart, 7

honesty and trust, 114, 128–129

HOW statements, 133–145

and imaginative acts (OWN IT!), 118–120

sales commitment, 200–201

service vs. price, 119

standing alone, 123–132

and uncommon offerings (WHAT), 112–114

Peugeot Open Europe, 35–36

P&G (Procter & Gamble), 14–15, 159

Potential vs. current customers, WHO statements, 47, 55

Prescription to over-the-counter (OTC) medication conversion, 151–155

Price vs. service, persuasive strategies (HOW), 119

Procter & Gamble (P&G), 14–15, 159

Product life cycle, WHAT enhancement, 91

Profits, and Inside Advantage, 2–3

"Profound transformation," avoidance of, 3

Prospecting, 37–38

Publicis Groupe SA, 4
(*See also specific companies*)

Reckitt Benckiser PLC, 15

References, 36–37

Referrals, 35–36

Revenues, and Inside Advantage, 3

Roaring Fork restaurant, Arizona, 63–64

Rollins, Kevin, 78

Rx-to-OTC conversion, 151–155

Saatchi, Maurice, 41–42

Sales, 2–3, 200–201

Sample statements
HOW statements, 140–143
OWN IT! statements, 185–197
WHAT statements, 102–104
WHO statements, 52–53

Sandoz (Novartis), 6, 114–116, 151–155

Sceti, Elio Leoni, 15

Schwab, Charles, 77

Scorecard, imaginative acts (OWN IT!), 208

Scott, Ridley, 158

Service vs. price, persuasive strategies (HOW), 119

Siemens, 39–40

Similarity, of customers, 33–35

SKF, 117–118

Slogans vs. WHAT statements, 105

Southwest Airlines, 5–6, 87–89, 161–162

Standing alone, persuasive strategies (HOW), 123–132

Starbucks, 32

Step-by-step development
explosive acts, 184–185
HOW statements, 138–140
OWN IT! statements, 184–185
ubiquitous acts, 184–185
WHAT statements, 99–101
WHO statements, 49–52

"Stickiness," of customer to product, 56

STRATEGIC, 176–177

Strategic framework, 180
(*See also* Growth Discovery Process)

Strategy, defined, 144
(*See also* Persuasive strategies [HOW])

Strength, unexploited, 1–2
(*See also* Inside Advantage)

Swiffer Wet Mop, 14–15

T-Mobile, 121–122
Tactics, defined, 144
Taglines vs. WHAT statements, 105
Tangible benefits, 59–62, 83–93
Targeting core customers, 23–40
    customer evolution, 23–26
    employee core customers, 38–40
    endorsements, 36–37
    failed approach, 31
    gender, and similarity to existing
        customers, 34–35
    large numbers, 37–38
    mental picture, 17–18
    prospecting, 35–38
    references, 36–37
    referrals, 35–36
    successful approach, 32–34
    (*See also* Core customers [WHO])
Taurus automobile, 90–91
Tavist, 151–154
T.G.I. Friday's, 65–67, 92, 116
Theraflu, 6, 114–116, 151
Tiffany & Co., 176–177
TNT, 181–182
TomTom, 130
Tools for women, 74
Touch points
    core customers (WHO), 67–69
    imaginative acts (OWN IT!),
        174, 198–200
    uncommon offerings (WHAT),
        92–93, 99–100, 106
Toyota, 182
Triaminic, 27–29, 85–87, 126, 151,
    163–164
Trust, persuasive strategies (HOW),
    114, 128–129

Twain, Mark, 42

Ubiquitous acts, 173–178
    core customers, 174–175,
        177–178
    defined, 165, 174, 200
    quality of, 199
    step-by-step development,
        184–185
Uncommon offerings (WHAT),
    59–107
    business, defined and identified,
        59–62
    commodity products, 69–75,
        79–81
    in common offerings, 69–75,
        79–81
    and core customers (WHO), 21,
        25
    customer touch points, 92–93
    defined, 63
    emotional connections, 60–61,
        63, 83–93, 106
    Growth Discovery Process
        chart, 7
    identifying, 64–67
    irrelevance, addressing,
        90–92
    maintaining freshness, 83–93
    obsolete offerings, 90–92
    and persuasive strategies
        (HOW), 112–114
    squandering, and flawed offerings,
        67–69
    tangible benefits, 83–93
    understanding experience
        offerings, 60–62

Uncommon offerings (WHAT)
    (*continued*)
    vs. unique offerings, 63–64,
        75–79
    WHAT statements, 95–107
Unexploited strength, 1–2
    (*See also* Inside Advantage)
Unique offerings, 63–64, 75–79
U.S. Food and Drug Administration
    (FDA), 151–152

van Gogh, Vincent, 131
Victoria's Secret, 179
Vision vs. WHAT statements, 101

Wal-Mart, 10, 73, 179
Wall Street Journal
    core customers (WHO), 14–15,
        24, 31, 34
    imaginative acts (OWN IT!),
        175, 183–184
    persuasive strategies (HOW),
        123–124, 133
    uncommon offerings (WHAT),
        77–78, 90–91
WHAT statements, 95–107
    consulting example, 96–99
    creation overview, 95–96
    emotional connection, 106

FAQs, 104–107
goal of, 106
length of, 104–105
sample statements, 102–104
step-by-step development,
    99–101
vs. tagline or slogan, 105
(*See also* Uncommon offerings
    [WHAT])
WHO statements, 41–56
    basic ingredients, 54–55
    consulting example, 43–49
    creation overview, 20–23, 41–44
    current vs. potential customers,
        47, 55
    FAQs, 54–56
    goal of, 54–55
    length of, 55
    sample statements, 52–53
    step-by-step development, 49–52
    (*See also* Core customers
        [WHO])
Women (*See* Gender)

Yahoo!, 76

Zale, Morris, 128
Zales, 128–129
Zeta-Jones, Catherine, 122

ABOUT THE AUTHORS

Robert H. Bloom is a widely respected authority on business growth.

As an entrepreneur, he grew a local advertising agency into a successful national agency.

As U.S. Chairman and CEO of Publicis Worldwide, the centerpiece of the $4.6 billion global marketing services company, he helped craft and implement the growth strategies of some of the world's largest companies and brands. At Publicis, Bloom managed over 1,000 employees, 12 U.S. offices, and a roster of clients including BMW, L'Oréal, Nestlé, T.G.I. Friday's, Whirlpool, Zales jewelers, and T-Mobile.

He also directed the launch of numerous brands that have become household names, such as Southwest Airlines, Nestlé Juicy Juice, T-Mobile U.S., and Novartis's Theraflu and Triaminic.

He is currently advising firms of every type and size on their growth strategies.

Dave Conti is a writer and an editorial consultant specializing in business and self-help topics. He cowrote, with management guru Stephen H. Baum, *What Made jack welch JACK WELCH: How Ordinary People Become Extraordinary Leaders*. Based on interviews with 30 CEOs, the book examines experiences that are the foundation of success in business and in life.

Conti is the former executive editor of HarperBusiness, the category-leading business book imprint of HarperCollins Publishers, where he acquired and edited books by many distinguished authors. He was responsible for a #1 *New York Times* bestseller plus numerous national bestsellers on the *Wall Street Journal*, *BusinessWeek*, and *New York Times* business lists.

Before joining HarperCollins, Conti was editorial director of Business McGraw-Hill, where he helped create a multimillion-dollar publishing program.

© Julia M. Conti.